SUSTAINABLE STAFFING

SUSTAINABLE STAFFING

How "Thinking Green" Is Changing the Way the World's Leading Organizations Attract (and Keep) Top Talent

Theo Rokos and Greg Rokos
with Lizz Pellet

Avocado Press

Sustainable Staffing:
How "Thinking Green" Is Changing the Way the World's Leading
Organizations Attract (and Keep) Top Talent
Copyright © 2012 Theo Rokos and Greg Rokos with Lizz Pellet
Published by Avocado Press

For more information visit www.GreenJobInterview.com

Printed in the United States of America

Sustainable Staffing:
How "Thinking Green" Is Changing the Way the World's Leading
Organizations Attract (and Keep) Top Talent
Theo Rokos and Greg Rokos with Lizz Pellet

1. Title 2. Author 3. Business

Library of Congress Control Number:2012902080

ISBN 13: 978-0-615-59863-5

*The single most amazing part of this journey has been
the people. While there is a sense of satisfaction that comes
with turning an idea into a profitable business, it pales
in comparison to the humility felt when someone believes in
you and walks alongside you in your quest. So it is
these people, our family, investors, employees,
partners and customers that walk alongside us,
to whom we dedicate this book.*

TABLE OF CONTENTS

CHAPTER 7
Industry Experts Add
Their Insights 153

CHAPTER 1

Sustainable Staffing

As we get started, Theo Rokos will explain what you can expect to gain from reading this book. You'll also get to learn who these writers are and what their backgrounds are.

Turbulence. The familiar bumping of the airplane had woken me up once again. I was hoping it was because the plane was touching down in Seattle. As I checked my watch I realized the plane would not land for another two hours. Fortunately for me I was on an aisle seat, the next best thing to being upgraded to first class. In those days, because of my airline status, I was usually upgraded about 50% of the time. The ball, however, did not bounce my way that night as I flew from New York to Seattle.

There I sat in my airline seat made for a nine-year-old. Next to me sat what appeared to be another veteran of the friendly skies, a business traveler no doubt. Those of us who have flown more than 100,000 miles in a year can spot each other. We are highly organized when sitting down—book, laptop, smartphone, water, and something to eat all neatly crammed into the storage area of the seat in front of us. In addition, many of us have developed the thousand-yard stare. This has been brought on by airline bag policies, groping TSA agents, and high-sodium airport food. While the majority of people on the plane are sleeping or watching a movie, we are at our office.

There is an unwritten code among frequent business travelers not to speak to each other unless both sides make eye contact and neither is in the middle of anything. This code has been created by countless flights of sitting next to a vacationing grandmother and her undying desire to give you her family tree, generation by generation, in the span of one airline flight. I had one who didn't stop talking until I got to the hotel. (I paid for her cab and shared it with her, so don't judge!) The gentleman sitting next me had silently decided all hurdles for communication had been cleared, though I was still not 100% convinced we were at that point, and he began to speak. He had the confidence of a man who had just had four glasses of skunked white airline wine. The whole experience could go horribly for me; he could sell something business to business and, when I told him my title, the rest of the trip would be one long, nightmarish sales presentation. Or worse he could be one of those damn HR people. He would spend the rest of the flight telling me what a pain in the ass sales people and sales leaders were, how we didn't listen, broke all the rules, and made his life a living hell.

"Four corners," the man said, and it drew a chuckle from me. I had never heard it called that before, but I was indeed on a "four corners" trip. My trip started with a Monday-morning flight from Orange County to Atlanta, followed later in the week by an Atlanta–to–New York leg, followed by this Thursday flight from New York to Seattle. Mercifully I would land in Orange County late Friday night.

My whole trip was for recruiting. In Atlanta, I had an interview with a partnership manager whom I was trying to steal away from a competitor. In New York I had interviews with three sales manager candidates. Seattle was a tactic I used when I quickly needed to put feet on the street.

We would have three people from the company (usually a recruiter and two local sales managers) rent a meeting room in a hotel and bring in twenty to thirty candidates throughout the day. I usually had a good excuse to miss these. However, being I'm the team leader, I had to eat the dog food from time to time.

Out of twenty candidates we might find two or three. Over 50% of these people were identified in the first ten minutes as not being good fits. It was not always our team identifying them as a non-fit based on experience or some other factor, but oftentimes they were not screened properly and were looking for higher paying positions, etc.

All in all, the entire trip was a total time suck. However,

I am a hands-on leader, and there was just not a better way than to fly to all four corners of the country. It turned out the other businessman and I had a lot in common. We both worked for large, growing companies. I had started my own consulting company and ended up signing on with my first customer. I missed the thrill of building and being part of a team. The job was to take a loosely run team of 250 sales people and grow it to over 1,000 account executives who would cover all fifty states. My counterpart worked for a fast-growing hotel chain, and he was sent in to hire out the staff.

As we carried on our conversation, we got into the real nuts and bolts of team building and recruiting. The thing we kept talking about was "waste"—how much time, money, and effort were wasted; how many resumes had to be read; how screening processes were not effective; and how getting a candidate on the interview calendar for everyone who needed to sign off on his or her possible hire was next to impossible.

The man continued to carry on, but I drifted off. I kept thinking back to a conversation my brother and I had while I was at the airport. My brother Greg had been in recruiting for twenty years. He founded and ran his own executive search firm, The Rokos Group. His company placed high-level executives in hospital systems. Over 90% of the time these candidates had to travel for the interview process. Greg started using the FedEx Kinko's model in his business, which had a lot of moving parts. First of all, both the hiring manager and the candidate had to find a Kinko's. In extreme cases the candidate would drive three or four hours to find a FedEx Kinko's. Once there, the candidate and hiring manager had one hour to do a "live virtual interview." The cost was around $500. If everything fell into place, it was less hassle than the airport. However, the cost savings was not enough to dominate the interview space.

All of these things had been in Greg's head. He reached me at LaGuardia Airport and said, "There has to be a better way to recruit." We agreed to sit down and discuss it over lunch. That call would lead to us creating a company that is changing the way companies and candidates meet for the first time. Looking back at it, I can't help but wonder how many start-ups were created simply by people being sick of flying through LaGuardia.

The Green Thing

Of course, being human, we have polarized the "green" debate. I wouldn't classify any of us as tree-huggers. This book will balance the need for sustainability with the need to make payroll; we get the position you're in. However, none of us can continue to act like there aren't choices. Creating a healthier planet will come down to large organizations. The media often portrays companies as these droid-like monsters intent only on making shareholders happy. I have been around long enough to know there is more than a grain of truth in those sentiments. However, corporations, no matter how large, are just a group of people with a common goal. The green movement is no different. Let those on the radical left try to do their nonsense and those on the radical right do theirs. Let's look at the facts and implement the most cost-effective and sustainable solutions. It's all about common sense.

Growing up in and around Orange County, I did not need a lot of information to form my opinion on the human effect on the environment. The smog here is unreal, and you can literally live it and breathe it on many a day. The waters of the coast we grew up fishing in have been fished out. The water we used to swim in has been contaminated, and I don't let my children swim in the same spots in our bay where I did as a child. It is unfortunate "green" has torn us into multiple groups. I don't want to write one sentence that will contribute to any further debate. Anyone worth his or her salt realizes there are better ways to do things. Again, common sense.

Our promise to you is this book is not going to be political. If you don't like the word "green," then replace it with "pollution," "waste," or "sustainability." Do some reading on what the population on earth will be in 2050. If you don't think we're going to have sustainability issues, then there is no reasoning with you. If you think it's all a hoax, then you need to focus on the word "waste" and more specifically wasting money.

When we tore down the recruiting and Human Resources

function and determined how we could make it more green, we also came at it from a business perspective. We want this book to show how you can have a green HR and talent acquisition team, save your company green (money), and make more green (money). At the end of the day we are businessmen and business women, and we understand your company is always going to look for ways to save money and time. It was our job to find the solutions that did this and as a bonus make your HR function much more sustainable.

"Why is HR important in the 'green' movement?" I get this question all the time. I actually think HR is a huge key to the overall success of sustainability and the green movement. Corporations really run much of what goes on around the globe; they have a significant impact on governments and the decisions governments make; they have an enormous effect on individual employees, everything from where they live to what technology they use. Fixing the corporations will actually be the fastest and most efficient way to implement more-sustainable models of living and working.

If you decide to focus on fixing corporations, you need to decide where to begin. You need a division that touches every other division in the company. You also need to hire the right people and have the right corporate branding and messaging going out to ensure you are promoting sustainability.

HR has roots sunk into every part of a company. What

other divisions can handle this task? Sales? Let's get real; sales leaders are worried about quota. Period. HR is the best way to change or implement policies across a company. If we make the hiring process and HR processes sustainable, we then have the model and the environment to change the whole organization.

Who the Hell Are You?

This is the first question I always ask myself when reading a business book that claims to solve an issue or to make my company better. The beauty of this book is you get three distinct viewpoints. Greg is a recruiter who founded his own recruiting firm, I have built sales teams at three Global 5000 companies and have done it from the ground up in some cases, and Lizz Pellet is the Vice President, US for the Felix Global Corporation and our resident "expert" with a background in organizational change and employment branding.

My experience in executive-level management spans nearly a decade and is in a variety of areas. Formerly I served as the senior vice president of sales for the WorldPay Division of The Royal Bank of Scotland, and prior to that I worked for Wolters Kluwer and Scantron Corporation. I understand the political, implementation, and budget issues you face at your company. I have made a ton of mistakes I can help you avoid. I know better than most you need to have your ducks in a row at a big company. The message of the new philosophy or tool is key, and successful implementation requires timing and precision.

As I previously mentioned, Greg established The Rokos Group and served as its president. He's been working in the recruiting industry for twenty years and has already shared his expertise through many media interviews and while speaking at talent acquisition meetings for Fortune 500 companies.

Lizz is a thought leader in the HR space and has written two books, *The Cultural Fit Factor: Creating an Employment Brand That Attracts, Retains, and Repels the Right Employees* that was published by the Society for Human Resource Management (SHRM) in 2009 and *Getting Your Shift Together: Making Sense of Organizational Culture & Change*. She is also a Johns Hopkins University fellow as well as a professional educator, keynote speaker, facilitator, and certified National Speaker.

The three of us have a lot of combined experience. We don't know it all but are always trying to learn more. In the process of writing this book we created a place where companies and individuals could gather and share information—for free.

Please visit www.experiencepanel.com and sign up for our newsletter. We're really different from others in the space. Feel free to think of us as kind of a "Breakfast Club" group. We all come from different backgrounds and have successfully created a "green" company in the HR and talent acquisition space. This success has allowed us to see what companies all over the world are doing when it comes to sustainability in their HR processes. We want this book to give you tools you can implement today, and we will speak freely and openly. So thank you for reading the book, and we look forward to working with you.

Why Write a Book?

Other than to give our company a shameless plug, we actually were driven to write a book by our customer base and the feedback Lizz receives while speaking about how to get HR green at many of the national conferences . We often get the question, "What else can we do to be sustainable?" We had some good answers ourselves, but we really felt the timing was right to do the research and see what best practices we could discover. We also have a great deal of large companies using our services. While we have an excellent implementation team that does an excellent job of training and spreading the message, we felt we needed a better vehicle to spread the sustainability message and to promote virtual interviewing at the same time.

We don't pretend to know it all; no one does. However, throughout the book you will get expert commentary not only from us but from some of the finest minds in recruiting as well.

Don't Be a Tool

Throughout the following pages and chapters, Greg, Lizz, and I will lay out many options for you. Please keep in mind we are focused on eliminating waste, and wasting time in particular.

As in most industries, recruiting and HR have been overrun by technology. Some of the technology has been so advanced and gained so much market share companies have forgotten about treating their customers the right way. The market is also flooded with overengineered technologies that are wastes of time and will make your job more complicated. In addition, a complicated hiring process can turn off the best candidates.

In every suggestion, we make sure the solution passes a test, and we suggest you use it as well. Use what works for you and your organization. We don't have all the answers, and unlike other thought leaders we don't speak in absolutes. We do know one fact: things change—fast. Lizz will have the HR function broken down and has a set of philosophies she will share with you. Greg and I have one test we hope you take note of when recruiting or building teams of recruiters.

Get in Front of As Many "Passive" Candidates As Possible and Convince Them to Come and Work for Your Company

Be careful of tool overload. You want to be able to have as many opportunities as possible to close candidates and to be able to implement effectively. You also need to think about candidate experience. Always use your own experience as the paradigm. "Is this something I would be okay doing as a candidate?" It is very easy to adopt tools to make the hiring manager's job easier, but candidate experience should always be on your mind. Just because we can use tools does not mean we always should.

The goal of this book is to highlight how one small idea—live virtual interviewing—has a significant impact on sustainability. We hope you come away from this book thinking live virtual interviewing is the best thing since sliced bread. However, we realize hope is not a strategy. So at a bare minimum we know you'll come away from this book thinking about what you can implement at your organization to help save time, money, and of course, the planet.

CHAPTER 2

A Look Into the Future

Lizz, Theo, and Greg take a look at where HR and Talent Management will be heading in the future.

If you're still not convinced "going green" is here to stay, think again. Al Gore won an Oscar for *An Inconvenient Truth,* and Live Earth concerts have swept the globe. There is a 2011 book written by Paul Gilding, the veteran Australian environmentalist-entrepreneur, *The Great Disruption: Why the Climate Crisis Will Bring On the End of Shopping and the Birth of a New World.* He lays out some fascinating statistics and significant points to ponder, but he says the world is really in denial of the gravity of this crisis. My take after reading the outline of the book and introduction—I can only say *do the math.* Gilding cites the work of the

Global Footprint Network, an alliance of scientists that calculates how many planet earths we need to sustain our current growth rates. GFN measures how much land and water area we need to produce the resources we consume and absorb our waste using prevailing technology. On the whole, says GFN, with our current growth rate we are using up the earth's resources far faster than they can be sustainably replenished, so we are eating into the future. Right now, global growth is using about one and a half earths. "Having only one planet makes this a rather significant problem," writes Gilding.

Fortunately, environmental sustainability is developing as a promising key phrase in today's corporate world and will continue to creep into the minds of many organizations. Corporate strategy on environmental sustainability is basically designed by a company to provide a broader view of being a good corporate citizen.

The sustainability strategy focuses on the company's aim to improve and replenish the environment for the overall benefit of society. Moreover, the corporate sector functions in the way to connect both society and consumers at large. Corporate citizenship always refers to a company's contribution to the development of society and in turn the development of the masses. This contribution may be in the form of initiation of specialized environmental programs.

A May 2011 article by Tracey de Moresella appeared in Fast Company[1] and focused on the CEO's perspective

---

1   "CEOs See Sustainability As Engine For Growth But Industry Sectors Split On Priorities," Fast Company, http://www. fastcompany.com/1755330/ceos-see-sustainability-as-engine-for-growth-but-industry-sectors-split-on-priorities.

of the priorities in sustainability based on a study done by Accenture and UN Global Compact. This study revealed 93% of the 766 CEOs surveyed believed sustainability will be "important or very important" to the future success of their companies. One of the interesting things in this study was no one sector stood out as the leader in supporting sustainability. While energy, transportation, utilities, and automotive were very high, banking, communications, and consumer goods were just as strong. Peter Lacy, the managing director of Accenture Sustainability Services, stated "insights from the study have helped us to understand the executives' business lens for sustainability across all industries; we're starting to see signs of high performing business aligning sustainability with the top line."

We can agree corporate sustainability is an evolution on more-traditional phrases describing ethical corporate practice. Phrases such as "corporate social responsibility" (CSR) continue to be used but are increasingly superseded by the broader term "corporate sustainability." Unlike the other phrases focusing on "added on" policies, corporate sustainability describes business practices built around social and environmental considerations. This terminology is becoming common speak in the boardroom and the cafeteria, and it will continue to be a focus in all industries regardless of company size. No matter where the dialog about sustainability takes place, if this practice is not tied to organizational values, chances of this being woven into the fabric of organizational culture are slim. Values congruence is one of the most important drivers of a successful organization. Some forward-thinking companies have taken time to define their values in behavioral terms and woven the values into their performance-appraisal systems so everyone is held accountable for living those values.

One company taking this to heart is Boston Consulting Group (BCG), which ranked number two (up from number eight the previous year) in Fortune magazine's "100 Best Companies to Work For." What makes it so great?

The consulting giant not only avoided layoffs in the economic downturn but also hired its largest class of recruits ever in 2010. They're drawn by the firm's generous pay and a commitment to social work; its Social Impact Practice Network (SIPN) offers its employees a chance to work with the U.N. World Food Program and Save the Children, and BCG pulled its consultants off client projects to provide on-the-ground support in Haiti following the earthquake are a big social sustainability draw. These new recruits were motivated to join a company seriously committed to being a good corporate citizen, and if they do experience an authentic and congruent work environment, we can assume they will be more committed, engaged, and productive than in other organizations.

On the other side of that coin is BP. The British oil giant spent years building its image as an environmentally friendly company. That went up in smoke on April 20, 2010, when an explosion aboard the Deepwater Horizon drilling rig killed eleven workers and released a massive flow of oil into the Gulf of Mexico. At times the company seemed more exasperated by the problem than sorry about it. Then-CEO Tony Hayward resigned after making remarks the public found insensitive, including, "I would like my life back." The employees of that organization were embarrassed and demotivated by the handling of the crisis.

A 2009 report by The Sustainable Business Network of Washington (SB NOW) gives us a great list of why a company should go green: Their number-one reason?

1. **Increasing employee satisfaction, retention, and productivity**
2. Improving operational efficiency and effectiveness
3. Saving energy, water, and raw materials
4. Shielding the business from escalating energy and water prices
5. Branding the business and differentiating it from its competition
6. Developing a positive, proactive relationship with local compliance inspectors
7. Reducing pollution, waste, and greenhouse gas emissions
8. Avoiding fines

Does HR Have Its Head in the Clouds?

The answer is yes, but in a good way. Forty percent of HR executives surveyed by CIO Insight in 2010 planned to implement an SaaS solution for core HR needs by the end of 2011, with cost savings being the largest business driver of that decision. These cloud solutions are targeted to support talent management, recruiting, compensation, and workforce analysis to help their organizations become more strategic to the business and more valuable to the top and bottom lines.

William Clifford, Microsoft's chief environmental strategist, commissioned Accenture WSP Environment & Energy to analyze the energy use and greenhouse gas (GHG) emissions for on-premise vs. cloud-hosted deployments of three widely used Microsoft applications for e-mail, content sharing, and customer-relationship management. The study assessed the carbon footprint of server, networking, and storage infrastructure for three different deployment sizes (100, 1,000, and 10,000 users) and found the smaller the organization, the larger the benefit of switching to the cloud.

When small organizations (100 users) move to the cloud, the effective carbon footprint reduction could be up to a 90% savings by using a shared cloud environment instead of their own local servers. For large corporations, the savings are typically 30% or more. In a case study with a large consumer-goods company, the team calculated that

32% of energy use and resulting carbon emissions could be saved by moving 50,000 e-mail users in North America and Europe to Microsoft's equivalent cloud offering.[2]

HR organizations considering SaaS solutions should take into consideration both the industry they are in and the role of IT in their business models. There are four service models to consider as reported in the Oracle White Paper from April 2011, HR in the Cloud: Bringing Clarity to SaaS Myths and Manifestos. They are:

>**Private Clouds**—for exclusive use by a single organization and typically controlled, managed, and hosted in private data centers.
>
>**Public Clouds**—For use by multiple organizations (tenants) on a shared basis and hosted and managed by a third-party service.
>
>**Community Clouds**—For use by a group of related organizations wishing to make use of a common cloud computing environment, e.g., universities in a given region or branches of the military.
>
>**Hybrid Clouds**—When a single organization adopts both private and public clouds for a single application in order to reap the advantages of both.

---

2   "The Cloud's Green Advantage," Forbes.com, http://www.forbes.com/2010/11/12/energy-datacenter-enterprise-technology-cloud.html.

While we can function quite well with our heads in the clouds, the reality is there are so many solutions available to support HR professionals in their efforts to make their companies more-sustainable organizations and strategic business partners.

CHAPTER 3

A Simple Solution to a Complex Problem

To get things started, Theo and Greg will give you more insight into how virtual interviewing works. You'll also get to learn about GreenJobInterview.com's history and how it has grown and become the company it is today.

Company Challenges

In the business world, we as owners and managers are constantly faced with one challenge after another—there's no easy path to success. In order to be able to grow and increase our success, we have to be able to find out ways not only to meet each of these challenges head on but to also solve them so they don't hinder our work as we move forward. We have better things to do than to deal with the same problems multiple times.

Let's take a look at just a handful of the major challenges companies all over the world are faced with. We're sure virtually every business owner can identify with these.

Productivity

Every business is always looking for ways to be more productive. After all, isn't productivity directly linked to how well our business does overall? The more productive we are, the more business we can take on. And the more business we can take on, the more money we're able to earn in the end.

For example, if you run a restaurant, you want to make sure all the food is prepared in a reasonable amount of time so customers get served in a timely fashion. The sooner one set of customers is able to finish eating, the sooner you can seat more customers, and serving more customers will translate to more revenue for your restaurant. You'd have to be crazy to want things to take longer, serve fewer clients, and make less money.

Another benefit to being as productive as possible is getting repeat business. Restaurant patrons who feel they've been treated well and served quickly are more likely to return than customers who had to wait and don't want to waste time sitting and waiting again. The well-treated patrons are also more likely to recommend that restaurant to others, and with just about everyone living in a "social village" online, such recommendations have become more important than ever before. (More on "social" later.)

Making a good impression on those we serve is the key to making sure they will continue to choose to do business with us; if they have a negative experience, they're going to give a different company a try. Creating good experiences is also a way to possibly get more business as word of mouth does its job. Referrals can be an important part when it comes to building up a strong client base in business or recruiting.

One of the top goals of any business is to be as efficient and productive as possible. No one wants to deal with a company that doesn't have its act together, as that has a negative impact on the purchase decision. Every business wants people to walk away with the best image of it as possible, an image of a place where they want to work someday.

This good impression can benefit you in your hiring process. Potential employees might take note of how productive your company is and how much everyone in your company cares about doing a good job, and this could increase their desire to work for you. Early in my career I was recruited by a large company to build out a nationwide sales force. The hiring process was completely disjointed; I had to make four separate trips to the East Coast to interview with four different people. The company had major communication issues with hiring. I ended up taking the job, but I realized these communication issues were not isolated to the hiring process. HR and recruiting can assist the company in many ways. If the communication is solid around the hiring process, it can start a chain reaction in a company. I was too young and inexperienced at the time to recognize the red flags, but a more experienced candidate would have noticed this and turned down the job.

Saving Money

The need to save money is of paramount importance to any business. We don't want to be wasting our money by spending it on nonessential costs, so we always have to be on the lookout for ways to reduce our costs without hurting the quality of our services. Wasteful spending is one of the biggest mistakes people can make whether professionally or personally.

Any good businessperson knows you have to keep a close eye on the books at all times. Look at what you're spending your money on; is all of it really necessary? Are you possibly using your dollars for things that aren't really vital to your company and its operations? And are there any areas where you might be able cut costs? Are you spending more on your recruiting practices than is actually necessary? Can you still attract high-quality candidates while spending less on recruiting them?

These are all good questions to ask yourself, but just make sure you pay attention to the answers. If the answers show there are improvements to be made, take action; don't ignore what might need to be done to correct any problems.

By scrutinizing your expenses you will identify areas

where you can make a real difference in your business spending habits. We all want to see our expenses go down so our revenues go up. Let's be honest; we're in business to make money, not to give it all away to other people.

- It's not easy to save money when you don't know what you're spending. Take my word for it: some of the most well-respected companies in the world have no idea what their costs are for candidate travel. The problem is these expenses usually get billed to so many divisions no one has a good handle on them. Walk into the CFO's office and ask him or her to work with you to come up with the actual cost of candidate travel throughout the entire organization. Any CFO who would see the opportunity to reduce this figure by up to 75% is usually going to act on that information. The same goes for the opportunity costs associated with cost per hire (CPH).

Cost per Hire, Time to Fill, and Cost Ratio.

- This can be very difficult to bench-mark between industries, regions, and demographics.
- Most CPH calculations do not take into consideration the opportunity costs or risks associated with not filling the position.

- Example: Annual costs = $1,000,000 (at budget)
  - # of hires = 500
  - CPH = 1,000,000/500 = $2,000
- Cycle time or TTF (time to fill) is calculated from the date of the requisition to the date of hire or start date. This is hard to calculate because it is dependent on your culture and hiring practices.
- Time ratio (TR) is established by dividing the TTF by contracted TTF. This determines the number of days negotiated between the recruiter and hiring manager. This places the onus on both individuals and creates dual accountability. It is much like an earned run average in baseball.
- Average annual salary of new hires
- Recruiter work load (number of requisitions they have per week, month, quarter, year)
- Screening ratio—interviews to hire
- Acceptance rate
- Source utilization

Saving money is a huge topic at this time. As time passes and the job market turns, this will become less of a focus. It is important for us all to remember these times. The key is to learn to run lean even in the best of times. Save the money in hiring so you don't have to do layoffs in the future.

Hiring-Time Reductions

We all know when we need to fill a position, we want to get the right person as quickly as possible; the longer it takes us actually to fill the position, the longer our company is strained by either having the work put on hold or by having it done by another employee. We don't want to use more of our time than necessary to hire someone. Time spent hiring means time not spent performing other important company functions. If we can streamline the hiring process and make it quicker, we can get back to completing some of our additional duties sooner and feel relieved knowing we selected the right candidate to fill our open position.

Some of the biggest challenges both recruiters and hiring managers have is getting time on calendars and coordinating everyone's schedule to make the most efficient use of an interview. Another significant waste of time is having to go through a decision maker who needs to sign off on every last candidate.

Increasing Our Candidate Pool

When we're hiring, the last thing we want is a limited candidate pool. The most talented people who would be the biggest assets to our company could be in a different state or different country. We don't want to exclude these people from our search; we want to get them involved in it. Why settle for whoever is closest? With the advent of technology we can cast a wider net on the candidate pool, extending our reach and our offers to more people. Technology is a huge part of our lives; we can barely handle not being in constant contact with others through the use of text messages, instant messages, e-mails, and phone calls. We can have everything right at our fingertips with smartphones or other easily portable gadgets.

So why not use technology to our advantage even more than we already are? There's no reason not to use tools such as videoconferencing to meet initially some of those potentially great employees who might otherwise be excluded from the interview process. Live virtual interviews allow you to have the same experience as if they were sitting in your office. You can observe body language, ask follow-up questions, and carefully watch their responses to off-the-cuff questions. This live experience is not something you can get with some of the recorded video options. Sure, some of you are asking, "What does EEOC have to say about live virtual interviews? Isn't it discriminatory to base your hire decision on seeing the person?" The answer is live virtual interviews are the exact same experience as having candidates sitting across from you in your office, a coffee shop, or the board room. The only difference is you can't shake their hands or walk them to the door.

The good thing about live virtual interviews is if you have ever had the experience of flying a candidate in and realizing in the first twenty minutes he or she is not a good fit, you will realize it is easier to end a phone call than it is an in-person interview, especially if you have the candidate scheduled to meet with three or four other people in your organization or a scheduled dinner or lunch. It's much easier to break the ties quickly before investing a lot of time in that candidate. Live virtual interviews also give candidates opportunities to ask questions, and the best candidates are those who interview you as well.

Gaining a competitive edge has always been an important part of business, and technology can play a significant role in this. At this moment almost every industry has a large candidate pool, but times will change. There will be another talent war, and it is best to be prepared.

On top of that, live virtual interviews are the right thing to do. It seems as though concern for candidate experience and employee happiness has fallen by the wayside at many firms, and this will ultimately be their undoing.

Recruitment Strategy Development— Impressive Interviewing[3]

(Posted by Bill Humbert on October 5, 2009, at 2:30 p.m.)

You can imagine what a daunting task it is to write a blog on a topic that has generated enough books to pave the way from St. Louis to San Diego. However since this blog is another in the series of high-level blogs on Recruitment Strategy Development, it must be done.

---

3   "Recruitment Strategy Development—Impressive Interviewing," RecruitingBlogs, http://www.recruitingblogs.com/profiles/blogs/recruitment-strategy-6.

Is interviewing taken seriously in corporate America? If it were, hiring managers would be trained to be more effective in the interviewing process. As a matter of fact, trained and "certified" hiring managers from every company function would be involved. For instance, there would a certified interviewing manager in accounting, another in marketing, another in sales, etc

If Executives truly understood the cost of hiring the wrong person for a job, they would require the same or greater due diligence on the selection of a new employee as they require on the selection of a new corporate acquisition. This due diligence would include a meaningful job description, a meaningful interviewing process, and meaningful due diligence on the selected candidate after the interview (the subject of my next blog).

Let's examine the cost of hiring the wrong person. The first assumption is that they are in the position for 2 years before they make the grievous mistake that gets them fired (after being put on plan). Let's say that person is earning $60,000 per year plus full benefits (that they take Full advantage of!—especially the medical/dental insurance). They are in a decision making position, possibly team leader. Let's also say they have some client contact (customer service is full-time client contact). Does this begin to sound like someone your company has hired?

What are your "hard costs" of this hire? Did you pay a recruiting fee, relocation, advertising for the position (Internet postings, newspaper, other), attend Career Fairs, etc.? Did you need to pay their expenses to interview in person? Did you need to call in an employment attorney prior to letting them go? If not, how about your own corporate counsel's time? Were you sued by the candidate for wrongful termination when they were let go?

Many companies will glance at their "hard costs" of letting someone go but never even consider their potentially catastrophic "soft costs."

Let's examine the "soft costs" of someone who has been in a position for 2 years but is only doing part of their job—and not doing that well. What is the cost of the work that is either not done—or done by another member of the team? What is the cost of their disruption to the team? What is the cost of the credibility of the manager for hiring someone like them? Have they driven away a customer? (There are certain companies with whom I will not do business any longer because they have poor customer service.) What is the cost of managing, coaching, correcting them? What was the cost of the time spent interviewing them?

Certainly potential candidates have heard rumors about their lack of work ethic. Has their employment affected your brand as an employer? How has that affected recruitment? I could go on and on—and so could you.

On one occasion I conducted an interview-training session with a small consulting firm. The attendees included the CEO and CFO. At the beginning of the session, I asked the previous questions. The table with the CEO and CFO estimated that the potential damage to the company could reach to $1 million over 2 years. Imagine hiring just 4 people like that over a couple of years. Potentially that could make the difference between profit and loss—or even between staying in business or going out of business. That is how important interviewing and selection skills are.

How does this impact your recruitment strategy? Would it be wise for your Executive leadership to back an interviewing training budget for your hiring managers this year? Once an Executive understands the potential negative impact of a poor selection, they may be willing to put more money in the due diligence part of the process. More importantly, once they understand the positive impact of the perfect hire, they may be even more willing to fund interviewing improvements.

Let's assume that your Human Resource department has used their sources to develop a couple of candidates for a midlevel position. What is your process to determine if they are truly qualified for the position? Have you created a Visio diagram of the process so it can be easily examined and explained to a new employee responsible for the interviewing process? To complicate things, it is important to remember that "Recruiting IS Sales." In any sales process, time works against you. The good news and the bad news is that in the United States people may choose to work for someone or not if they are selected. Therefore it is important to move the recruiting/interviewing process along. Like managers, few candidates have been trained in the interviewing process. Therefore, if they don't hear from you, they simply assume there is no interest and psychologically move on. Now you have lost that initial enthusiasm for your company and position.

When you create an interviewing process, it is a good idea for someone to do a phone screen on the candidate to determine if their skills and personality are a close enough match for your company. Why go through the time and expense of a personal interview if they clearly do not fit? If potentially they are a fit, then you create an interviewing team that will interview the candidate and then meet to discuss the person and give the thumbs up or down on them.

In the process, the hiring manager should be responsible for determining who should interview the candidate(s). Once the interviewing team is established, the hiring manager should ask the team members to focus on the aspects of the interview that are their strengths. It is a good idea for everyone to ask some set of the same questions, just to create a benchmark.

Let's take a few minutes to discuss the interview and the questions asked. In over 28 years of recruitment, my experience has shown that when you give a manager a list of questions without training them to listen to the response, they will focus on the next question instead of listening to the response of the candidate. That's not good. Train them to be active listeners. The response of the candidate will give them far more material to probe, and it will be more on target than any list of questions the managers can start with.

Technical skill interviews whether they are IT, medical, financial, accounting, etc., can be easier to measure than a person's motivation or cultural fit. You develop a "Test" with either right or wrong answers. Then you grade the responses. Set a level the person must pass in order to receive an offer.

In 1992, I was asked by MCI to develop a recruiting strategy to transition an IT group from Virginia to Iowa. We needed to recruit a minimum of 120 IT professionals to Cedar Rapids in 12 months. One of the Senior Managers suggested that we create a set of technical questions that we ask each programmer or programmer/analyst. We had a senior technical professional create the interview so that the answer was either right or wrong. Therefore we could grade them on technical knowledge. No matter how much we liked someone (the gut); if they did not score at least a 76, we would not extend an offer to them. As a result of our strategy and interviews we were able to recruit 133 professionals to Cedar Rapids in 12 months—and the technical team was able to get two new releases out on time. We may have been able to attract that number of people without the "test," but they may not have been able to get the releases out on time if their skills were not up to par.

That metric is much easier to measure than the one for cultural fit. Interviewing for cultural fit generally requires an in-depth behavioral interview with good follow on questions. Again, the temptation is to focus on the next question without hearing the response of the candidate. See the next example for the reason to listen.

In 1997, I was asked to begin to train a junior human resource Rep on interviewing. We decided to use an Executive Administrative Assistant position that we were recruiting for as the first step. She went through the resumes and forced ranked all of the resumes by how she felt they stacked up against the requirement. When I went through the stack, I ranked them roughly the same. Then I asked her to invite the top 3 candidates in for an interview. When the candidates came in, she introduced them to me. I thanked them for coming for the interview, explained that I was training the Rep to interview and that if we went through the entire interview without me ever asking a question, that's fine. It just meant that I followed what they said. However if I should ask a quick question, it only meant that I was a little confused about something. The first two candidates probably did not even realize I was in the room. They were fine.

The third candidate proved that active listening is important. The interview was going fine until the Rep asked the candidate what weakness she had (not my preference of words but it was on the table). The candidate said that her weakness was that she liked people too much. Well, that was the first time I had heard that weakness, so it really caught my attention. She went on to say that it probably really was a strength because it made her more effective. I thought, "Hmm, she has been coached." The Rep was going to let it go at that and began to ask the next question. I excused my interruption and asked if I could ask a question. The Rep said "Sure!" I looked at the candidate and said, "When you were asked about a weakness, you responded and turned it into a strength. That was fine, and I know that technique of coaching. However, what we really were looking for was what areas as an Executive Assistant could you improve?" She proceeded with, "Well another weakness is that I am…"and turned that into a strength. So I said, "Let's move away from weakness. If you were to come to work here, what kind of training could my client offer you to improve your skills?" Her response? "I Am Not a WEAK Person!!!" Wow! Probably not weak, but she doesn't listen and certainly was not a match for that VP. I apologized profusely. While the questions from the Rep continued politely, the interview was over—and she didn't realize it.

Humans are wonderful beings. Like it or not, we are also somewhat predictable. Generally if we have found a way to succeed, we continue to use that same behavior time and again. That is the basis of behavioral interviewing. We may stop if we were a total failure using that method once but push come to shove, we will usually revert back to the original behavior while under stress.

Develop situations in your company that this person may face and ask them how they responded to a similar situation in a previous company. Those answers will help you determine if they are a good fit. Ask them about previous successes and failures and what they learned from each. After you ask a few additional questions, circle back and create a situation in your company that is similar to one of their failures, and ask them how they would handle it.

Making notes during an interview is fine if it doesn't distract you too much (Never, never make notes on a resume and then save it!! When? Never!). The interview should be a conversation where you learn about each other and determine if the position is a good mutual fit.

When the interview is done, the last person with the candidates should thank them for their time. Then ask them if they have any further questions or concerns. Do your best to be sincere and truthful. Remember, they may be a current or potential future customer. Once their questions are asked and answered, manage their expectations for the next steps of the process. If your company is very interested in them, be sure to let them know that also. Remember this is the needs analysis step of the sales process for both the candidate and the company.

Within 24 hours the team needs to discuss the candidate(s) and determine if there is further interest in them. If there is interest, it is best to begin the post interview due diligence—and possibly generate a contingent offer based on the outcome of the due diligence.

The RecruiterGuy summary: document your interview process. Train your managers to become effective interviewers. Develop interviewing teams for each open position. Develop "technical tests" that must be passed. Develop a good behavioral interview for the cultural and motivation parts of the interview. Make the initial hire/no hire decision after the interviewing team meeting. Extend a contingent offer if this is the right person. Begin the post interview due diligence—drug test, background investigation, reference check by the hiring manager, and psychological assessment if required.

We want to make sure those candidates we are considering bringing onboard have the best experience possible. After all, isn't the hiring process the first insight people get into our company? First impressions are important, and we don't want to lose out on potential talent by not giving the best first impression we can and not putting our best foot forward.

Instead, we want those talented people who will be an asset to our company to walk away from the process feeling impressed and confident. We want them to leave hoping they'll be the person we hire and looking forward to coming back to work for us.

It's not just the candidate who has to make a good impression—it's us too. The better we make the experience for potential hires, the more they'll realize how we feel about those who work for us, namely, we value them and think they are valuable to our companies. We want to show we don't take any employee for granted.

By using virtual interviewing and helping eliminate candidate travel, you are demonstrating to your candidates that the work-life balance is something your company respects. It will also show them you are progressive, innovative, and a friend of the environment.

The candidate experience will also be improved by cutting out the stress some candidates feel when they have to figure out scheduling travel to make it to an interview. Having to balance family schedule with work schedule and interview schedule can be a difficult task. They are sure to appreciate that you've actually taken into account how you can give them a far better experience during this experience.

One of our health-care clients won an award for best candidate experience at the global ONREC conference in 2010. Here are the award criteria and our client's award submission; this will give you a sense for the business case for using GreenJobInterview.com and the actual candidate experience when using this live virtual interview solution.

Category: Best Candidate Experience

Name of campaign:
Live virtual interviews with GreenJobInterview.com

Organization/agency name:
Health System

Name of organization's/client business/industry:
Health care

Campaign team leader title:
Regional Director Physician Recruitment
Vice President Physician Integration

Relevant team members and job titles:
Physician Recruiter
Physician Coordinator

Background: Provide details of the business and the recruitment requirement that prompted development and/or implementation of the effort.
Our Health System is a 5-hospital healthcare system in an area that has experienced rapid

population growth over the last few years, which has significantly increased the demand for additional physicians to serve the community. A major priority identified in our 2009/2010 strategic plan was the need to recruit 71 additional physicians to the service area. Given the national physician shortage and fierce competition from other health systems, we needed a recruitment strategy to differentiate itself from the competition and attract the best physician talent.

Strategy: Describe the campaign, detailing the different elements, solution, tools or media used, and why each was used. What was the strategy and how did it fit the objective(s)? In what ways was it innovative?

Goals:

1. Differentiate us from the competition by creating a better candidate experience.
2. Leverage technological advances to improve candidate vetting process and create a branding platform which allows us to tell our story.

Recruitment Tool: Live virtual interviews in a branded meeting room:

Innovation: Very few health systems use this technology to attract top physician talent, which made it ideal for helping differentiate us from the competition and create a more compelling candidate experience.

Effectiveness: How successful was the campaign? It was very successful. We met our recruitment goal for the fiscal year. We're particularly pleased with our successful physician recruitment in the 25–34 age group as these physicians were a key target audience. Equally important were the improvements in our candidate vetting (screening) process and how we were able to use the technology to differentiate us from our competitors. Physician and staff testimonials confirm the impact of this tool on both our leadership and our physician candidates. In addition to helping lower our cost per recruit, we've been able to showcase our culture and values to prospective candidates more effectively. The unscripted, free-flowing communication platform allows us to spotlight our physician leaders and hospital executives and describe our day-in-the-life practice opportunities with more passion and enthusiasm. Because of the ease of scheduling interviews, fewer physician candidates have dropped out of the process, which has contributed to a more robust candidate pool.

(Candidates often drop out of the process when there is such a time lag in coordinating schedule and those of physician leaders involved in the recruitment process.)

What measures were used to gauge its effectiveness? Provide quantifiable evidence of how the campaign helped the recruitment objectives.

- Increased opportunity to showcase our system
- Lower cost per recruit
- Lower candidate drop-out rate
- Faster time to fill positions

Your view: Why should the judges give this entry an award?

MD comment: "I had a hundred opportunities to consider and only a finite number of days and weekends in my residency training when I could go on a site visit. The Systems use of GreenJobInterview.com really impressed me. I thought, 'If this organization is using this advanced technology in the interview process, they must be technologically advanced in their hospitals as well.' I am a hospitalist, so this is important to me and my patients. Video interviewing was a great time saver and so easy to use. It definitely differentiated this opportunity from all the others."

Vice President Physician Integration: "So much of good communication is in body language. Being able to see a candidate's facial expressions and body language is extremely helpful as these clues are a good indication of what our patients would see as well. GreenJobInterview.com reveals so much more than we could ever discern on a phone call. Our team is able to observe how a candidate interacts in semi-stressful situations like a job interview before we incur all the travel costs associated with a site visit. It's a very valuable recruiting tool for our company."

GreenJobInterview.com—Our History

GreenJobInterview.com was created to help address and solve the challenge of the first interview. There is some confusion in the space around terminology, but we feel it is very simple. A one-way recorded process in which a candidate answers questions and the responses are stored is not an interview. Any recruiter worth his or her salt will tell you the most important part of any interview is the questions the candidate asks the company. Through our collective years in the industry we've seen the hardships companies face, and we understand where they're coming from. We also know what it takes to overcome hurdles and make improvements.

We founded GreenJobInterview.com in 2007 with the

idea of having companies and job seekers alike start to see the way face-to-face interviews could be conducted in a whole new way. We wanted to get them thinking past having physically to see each other in person for there to be a face-to-face interview. They needed to realize there are other ways actually to see someone.

Through technological advancements and the development of personal computers, webcams, and the Internet, you don't need to be in the same room as someone to be able to see him or her while you're speaking. These technological devices let both the recruiter and the candidate view each other on a screen and speak to one another, making it a great alternative to meeting in person.

Our goal was to eliminate completely the need to travel when companies were conducting their first round of interviews for any position, and we did so by putting all of these ideas together and using technology. Plain and simple, it didn't make sense to do so much traveling for first-time interviews. We have a philosophy of keeping things simple and comfortable for the candidate, and that's why on 95% of interviews we use the phone instead of voice over IP (VOIP). Why? It's easier and it's better. Wearing a headset during an interview is uncomfortable, to say the least, and VOIP is not nearly as clear and consistent as the telephone. Again, it's so easy now it makes no sense not to conduct first interviews in this fashion.

Others in the industry have agreed. Fi Haywood of Virtual Interview Lounge once wrote, "Putting candidates on a plane, train, or automobile when you have a perfectly good web-based video technology accessible from your desktop in less than a minute to conduct first-round interviews seems ludicrous; that's because in this day and age, it is ludicrous."[4]

We also wanted to create a positive videoconferencing experience that actually offered customer service rather than people just being thrown in a room with the equipment and needing to fend for themselves.

But we didn't want to be just a green company; we had more in mind for how we would define our business. Although being green was and is important to us, we wanted to create tools to make life easier for recruiters and hiring managers alike. Finding the right people for your company can be a difficult and complicated process. The status quo was crazy and just wasn't working, so we wanted to come up with industry solutions that made far more sense.

In the very beginning of GreenJobInterview, there were two functions we were doing—video resumes and video interviewing. Through www.futureresume.com, people were able to submit a virtual resume. These job seekers would record one-minute speeches detailing their work histories for potential employers. The problem was the candidates could not ask the company any questions. The best candidates are usually passive in that they are currently

---

4   "Creating a Successful Virtual and Video Interviewing Strategy," HubPages, http://fihaywood.hubpages.com/hub/Video-Interviewing-Strategy.

employed and not necessarily looking, and they typically have lots of questions. It's not convenient for passive candidates to record anything, and at a certain level people are going to say, "No way" to having a recording of themselves floating around a company and being shown to whomever the company deems fit. Think about yourself for a moment; imagine you walked into a recruiter's or a decision maker's office and he or she had a video recorder set on a tripod and asked you, "You don't mind if I turn this on and record our conversation, do you?" I'm not sure how you would respond, but I'd say "No thank you." If the recruiter insisted and said it was company policy or part of their culture, I'd say "No thank you. I obviously wouldn't be a good fit here… Have a nice day."

However, some companies do record interviews, and it serves them well. Many organizations are using recorded interviews in campus recruiting or when they are recruiting a large number of entry- or lower-level candidates. This process can save a lot of time in the elimination phase of filling these types of positions. But our philosophy is certain conversations in life don't need to be recorded, and an interview is one of them. As recruiters, we could never get our arms around the shelf life of these videos. For example, at one point in my career I was an account executive, and eighteen months later I was a director with an MBA. We aim to be more on the "service" side of the equation. We want to be the company you use for higher-level virtual interviews.

When it has to go right, we want the call. However, as stated, there is a place for the recorded resume, and we partner with companies that do excellent jobs of providing them.

The first thoughts about futureresume.com morphed into live virtual interviews, which grew into GreenJobInterview.com. The more we had read about sustainability, the more we felt this tool could have a dramatically positive impact on the environment by reducing carbon footprint.

GreenJobInterview is growing at a fast pace and doing so in the midst of a recession during which job creation is not a happening thing. Many industry leaders and Fortune 500 companies have recognized the value of this solution. We believe the driver to reduce cost per hire logically leads forward-thinking companies to try something new, and once they tried it, it stuck and has become best practice for these organizations.

We had to deal with many typical start-up business challenges, such as having limited capital, finding the right people to work with us (often at a reduced market value with hopes of a greater return) and creating messaging, processes, and systems. It also took a lot of work for us to figure out how to get our message out to potential clients. Finding the right fit for us was kind of easy—we were direct, we clearly articulated our goals, and we gave these individuals a chance to be a part of a "game changer" in the industry.

Getting our value proposition out was a bit harder. We knew we had found a solution that was better than the status quo—but now we had to get potential buyers to understand that and stay still long enough to listen to our story. Those potential buyers were recruiters, hiring managers, and talent acquisition directors. It was imperative to get those people to take a look at what we were trying to do because without them making use of this solution we wouldn't have been able to get into the game.

We also had to get people to understand there is a high level of anonymity with a live virtual interview. They were very confidential, and none of the interviews would end up on the Internet or posted on YouTube. People had to be confident their privacy would be protected at all times.

We're happy to say we were able to get people to listen, so much so we have become the de facto standard for interviewing in a good number of the top Fortune 100 companies. Some of these companies have realized the value of conducting virtual interviews in the initial screening process and have policies in place specifically stating a person cannot fly a candidate in for an interview without first conducting a GreenJobInterview. We think that says a lot for our solution.

We understand as an HR professional you want to make a valuable investment in your business by hiring the right person. But we also know you don't have to spend a huge amount of money on traveling expenses to do so. GreenJobInterview gives you the opportunity to take part in live virtual interviews with candidates. This way you can have that face-to-face experience by taking advantage of technology and without having to spend a lot of money on getting the person physically to your office.

While accomplishing this, there are a lot of things we strive to do for those we work with. First of all, we treat everyone with respect and compassion in a very professional manner. We value all the people we work with, whether partners, clients, candidates, or employees. We show this by treating individuals the way they deserve to be treated. We never want anyone to feel he or she is just another person or client; we want everyone involved in the interview process to feel relaxed and prepared. This is one of the reasons we conduct a "tech check" prior to the interview with every candidate, hiring manager, or recruiter. This is not like Skype, which uses a third-party vendor to take your personal information, offers no technical support, and is conducted on a nonencrypted site. How many times have you started a call or videoconference and fumbled with technology for the first ten minutes? We consider that to be a waste of valuable time. We check viewing camera presence, lighting, environment, and any technical issues that might arise due to Internet speed or lack of technical knowledge, like how to plug in a USB. Don't laugh! We've had some very high-level people who had never heard of a USB. We have also had candidates who had some pretty interesting things going on behind them or framed on their wall. We like to provide this tech check so it is almost exactly the same as the candidate being in your office. The tech check ensures that there is no fumbling with technology at the time of the actual interview. We want to make sure the candidate and the hiring manager or recruiter are prepared and their virtual experience is much like their meeting live in an office setting for the interview.

GreenJobInterview is also more than a business just trying to make money. It's imperative to us that we are able to give back to our communities. We feel it's necessary to be active members of the communities in which we live and work so we can help make them better for ourselves and for others as well. Because of this, we donate some of our profits to other organizations, specifically to those working toward reducing corporate environmental impacts.

Our commitment to assisting our communities has included being involved with local groups working to keep our oceans and beaches clean. We also make it a point to sponsor activities we are personally connected to, such as the Little League or other sports teams our children might be involved in. In general, we try to rotate whom we donate to so we can help a variety of organizations. Why mention this? If anything, to remind you to not be trying always to get to the top of the mountain. Please reach down and help others up. Being a sustainable society will ultimately require us all to pitch in and help out where we can.

In addition to supporting other organizations that help our planet, we take a hands-on approach to making a difference in the area of being green and sustainable. Much of this is accomplished through word of mouth and talking to others about what they can be doing to make a difference. We also make sure to share helpful information we come across as much as we can. For instance, we frequently post information on green activities to our Facebook page so others can benefit from that knowledge. In early 2011 we started a LinkedIn group dedicated to providing information on sustainability as it relates to HR. In six months we had over 3,000 professionals join. It is called LinkedHR Green, if you'd like to join.

We do what we can to encourage others to become more environmentally conscious and sustainable, including through our daily work of keeping people off of airplanes. It will take all of us doing our part to make a real difference in protecting our planet. For us, it's not enough to lead by example; we also have to get the word out to other businesses that there's still more to be done so they can join us in making big changes.

One of the reasons for the successes of GreenJobInterview is we come from "bottom line" backgrounds. As owners and employees of companies whose sole concern was generating revenue, we know saving time and money while increasing productivity will always be held in higher esteem than sustainability, and that's not something we're likely to see change.

But sustainability doesn't have to be ignored. Entrepreneurs can find ways to fulfill our goals while also being environmentally conscious, and HR professionals can be a big part of it too. We can play a major role in getting other businesses involved, showing them there is real value in creating practices and policies within HR, and proving we can be a leading force in these sustainability initiatives.

Through our work at GreenJobInterview, one of the things we strive for is to help you meet the challenges we wrote about earlier. We can help you make a big difference in those areas so your business can move forward in a positive way. We will also help you rest easier, knowing you're doing all you can to help your company.

SHRM Survey

Information from the Society for Human Resources Management (SHRM) really helps show where companies are currently at with their green business practices. In May 2011, SHRM, along with BSR and Aurosolorya, released its report, "Advancing Sustainability: HR's Role." To compile the information, SHRM surveyed more than 1,700 HR professionals beginning in February 2010.

The report began by pointing out "no matter what your personal opinion might be, business leaders are realizing sustainable workplace and business practices can make their companies more competitive in the 21st century."

As companies continue to work toward being even greener in the future, SHRM noted those in the HR field are "uniquely positioned to be a catalyst" in helping all these changes come to fruition.

But where exactly do companies stand now when it comes to their sustainability practices?

SHRM found 68% of businesses were using at least some form of a sustainable workplace or business practice, while 28% were not.

One reason why these businesses might be employing green policies has to do with their return on investment. Of the 39% of business calculating their sustainability efforts' ROIs, according to SHRM, 47% found their ROIs were positive. Another 46% said it was too early to tell, while 6% said so far they had only broken even. However, SHRM noted none of the companies had reported having negative ROIs.

Through its recently released report, SHRM examined the motivations behind making investments in sustainability programs. Of the survey respondents, 39% cited the ability to make societal contributions, 13% said it was to gain a "competitive financial advantage," 12% noted considerations for the environment, 10% said it was to save on their operational costs, and 8% said it was because of health and safety concerns.

SHRM reported two factors were important to the success of implementing sustainability programs. First, the organization said it's necessary for the top executives to be supportive of the efforts. In addition, having other employees within the business who value sustainability can make a big difference.

SHRM pointed out how some of the benefits of being sustainable could lead employees to want to support them.

As SHRM wrote, "Organizations can leverage sustainability to attract, retain, and develop employees." Because all these factors can contribute to the overall success of a business, they give individuals in the company reasons to support the programs.

Just some of the other positive outcomes reported by survey respondents were improving morale of employees, the efficiency of their business processes, employee loyalty, brand recognition, and employee retention.

Since the above areas are all directly part of the work done by HR professionals, it would make sense for them to be involved in sustainability programs. However, SHRM found only 6% of HR departments were responsible for creating these strategies, while 25% were responsible for their actual implementation. SHRM said sustainability efforts are "a call to action for the HR profession to take a greater role in the strategic planning process and display leadership on this important topic."

Although there may be many benefits to introducing these policies, SHRM found organizations face a variety of barriers in doing so. The top five were launching costs, difficulty measuring ROI, a lack of support from the organization's leaders, costs related to maintaining the programs, and an absence of the knowledge or capacity needed to implement the programs.

There may be some challenges to overcome, but HR professionals could play an important role in overcoming them. As the SHRM report concluded, "the HR profession is and will continue to be an important component in the emergence and evolution of sustainability."

What the Numbers Show

For many businesspeople, numbers speak louder than words. So let's take a look at some of these numbers, which really help illustrate why it's such a good idea to use live virtual interviews.

In the past, it could cost you as much as $500 an hour to go to a FedEx or Kinko's to use its videoconferencing equipment. When FedEx converted to FedEx Office, it still did not provide any support for the videoconferencing product. If the video was not working, you had to wait in line behind someone ordering copies or wedding invitations before you could get a service representative to try to help you fix the equipment. FedEx instituted a fix for this waiting period and hired an external vendor to oversee its video operations, but this proved to be a very costly service for FedEx, and as of August 2011 it started phasing out videoconferencing at all of its locations.

The average in-person interview can cost $1,200 to $1,500, and that's just for travel and transportation. Add in meals and hotel, and the figure can be over $2,000, depending on where you are located. The amount for a live virtual interview with GreenJobInterviews could be as little as $129 for unlimited time per interview. For the videoconferencing model, there are no bridge fees or additional user fees. Saving more than $1,000 per interviewee can add up quickly. We have worked with Fortune 500 companies that have been able to save millions by making the switch to live virtual interviews.

> *People wake up! You've got a company that, if it were a country, would be the twentieth biggest in the world, pledging to be the world's largest organic retailer, and to be carbon neutral. This is the fall of the Berlin Wall in sustainability. This is a complete sea change.*
>
> —L. Hunter Lovins[5]

We came across this quote in Force of Nature: The Unlikely Story of Wal-Mart's Green Revolution, by Edward Humes. We believe this is the most important book ever written on the topic of corporate sustainability. Humes bridges the gap between profits and sustainability and shows how Walmart was smart enough to figure out sustainability is a better and more efficient set of goals. By thinking of sustainability at every turn, you will actually add to your bottom line.

Walmart's total 2010 annualized savings was $2 million, consisting of 145 live virtual interviews a month. From January to December 2010, Walmart conducted a total of 1,735

---

5   L. Hunter Lovins and Boyd Cohen, PhD., Climate Capitalism: Capitalism in the Age of Climate Change (Hill and Wang, 2011).

live virtual interviews. Had these interviews been done in person, Walmart would have spent around $2,206,000. The cost breakdown for Walmart to conduct 191 interviews alone was $133,700 for air travel, $19,100 for ground travel, $38,200 for lodging, $28,650 for meals, and $9,550 for additional miscellaneous expenses.

However, by doing them virtually instead, they spent only $223,594.63, a savings of more than $1.9 million. They must have been overjoyed to be able to save that much money and very happy with their recruiters for helping to make it all happen.

By turning to GreenJobInterview.com, Walmart was able to help itself in two big ways. First of all, it gave itself the opportunity to build on something it holds important—being environmentally conscious. Based on its other practices, it's obvious Walmart wants to make a difference in helping the planet. By cutting down on flying in potential hires, Walmart was able to assist it even further and reduce the carbon footprint the company is leaving on the world.

In addition, it saved Walmart money. It was making a huge investment by having all those candidates travel in for interviews. Switching to live virtual interviews represents an incredibly sizable reduction in expenses while improving a company's ROI.

There is actually another upside to this, too. Taking advantage of this service also left a positive impression on those being interviewed. One candidate said, "I think it's great Walmart is thinking about the environment. I want to work for a company that thinks about the details."

Month	Live Virtual Interviews	In-person Interview (avg. cost $1,200)	Cost of Live Virtual Interviews	Total Savings
Feb. 2010	75	$90,000	$10,803	$79,196
March 2010	75	$90,000	$10,081	$79,918
April 2010	104	$124,800	$15,623	$109,176
May 2010	137	$164,400	$22,238	$142,161
June 2010	121	$145,200	$17,945	$127,254
July 2010	152	$182,400	$20,774	$161,625
Aug. 2010	238	$285,600	$27,230	$258,369
Sept. 2010	249	$298,800	$29,000	$269,799
Oct. 2010	168	$201,600	$20,029	$181,570
Nov. 2010	220	$264,000	$24,147	$239,853
Dec. 2010	145	$174,000	$17,974	$156,025
Jan. 2011	182	$218,400	$21,157	$197,242
Feb. 2011	182	$218,400	$19,634	$198,765
Total	**2048**	**$2,457,600**	**$256,641**	**$2,200,957**

Whether a company is small or large, there are savings to be had, and major savings at that. Financially it just makes sense. You can save money on your recruiting process while still bringing in quality talent.

We can talk about realized savings in hard-dollar costs with every client example we have, but there are many intangibles that are also positives. The winter of 2010 was particularly hard on the Midwestern and Northeastern states. Travel delays, flight cancellations, and harsh weather are also part of the candidate travel experience we need to consider. If you have ever been in Houston and the airport closes and all the retail outlets close and there is not an empty hotel room for thirty miles (with the exception of the Champion Inn on the airport service road, behind Hooters) and you don't know if you can get out on the first flight in the morning, you know the level of frustration cancelled flights can be.

CO_2 Emmisions

In-person Interviews   **Live Virtual Interviews**
645 kg CO_2   **17 kg CO_2**

What About Free?

We get questions about free services all the time. You can now get free e-mail from many different places. Is your company using these free e-mail services? Probably not. The main reason is service. With Skype and other free services there is little to no service. You also are going to create a poor candidate experience by using these. Your candidates are going to go to Skype and give it all of their information. Then they have to download Skype on their computers and get themselves up on camera. Then they are going to conduct an interview via VOIP. This is a very drawn-out and frustrating process for candidates. We had a Fortune 500 company try it; they signed up with us within three weeks. You will see why Skype is not the answer the minute one candidate does not have a webcam. If you're a small shop or a one-person recruiting outfit, then by all means do what you have to do. However, the reasons to use a video interview service are almost too robust to name, but here are a few:

- Security
- Service
- Custom branding
- Candidate experience
- Remaining friends with your IT department—it will become the candidate service provider if you choose this route

- Effective coordination
- Reporting

I will gladly refer you to any other service provider in the space before I would refer you to a free service.

Success Stories

Just like numbers tell a big story, so do tales of success other businesses have already had using GreenJobInterview.com. Who doesn't like to hear concrete proof? After all, it's all well and good for us to say how great we think our product is, but don't we also want to hear what the people who have actually made use of it have to say? In the coming chapters you'll get to read additional testimonials from some of our clients.

Brent McCombs—former vice president of talent management at Waste Management

It's no surprise Waste Management is one of those companies on the way to becoming greener. Their catchy Think Green tagline has been established for years. Brent McCombs, the former vice president of talent at Waste Management, talked about the green efforts in its HR practices. The HR team has done a lot of work around sustainability and recently moved to a greener office space. The virtual webcam interview solution is just one of the tools it is now using in its candidate selection process.

In 2009, Waste Management began looking at live virtual interviewing solutions. As the leader of providing environmental services in America, McCombs said the company is always looking for environmentally friendly ways to conducts its business. It also gets its employees involved in trying to come up with new ideas.

"We ask our 20,000 drivers to think green every day," he said. "If our workforce is committed to being green, that helps our employment brand and our organizational mission."

One of the ideas to come out of Waste Management's efforts to find additional green solutions was using virtual interviews.

"We found live virtual interviews were an excellent way to support the green initiative as well as provide a cost saving for us," said McCombs. "No one told us to go out and reduce cost in the hiring process, but when we looked at how easy this process was, the cost saving was an added bonus."

McCombs said by conducting virtual interviews before actually flying candidates in, Waste Management has been able to save about $1,000 per interview. McCombs said they conducted about 185 live virtual interviews in one year-and-a-half period, resulting in savings of $185,000.

"When you think about air travel, hotel, ground transportation, and meals, that all adds up very quickly. Plus, add in your staff time to coordinate and book the travel, conference rooms, and block calendars," he explained. "That can all be eliminated by deploying this solution."

The above aren't the only benefits Waste Management has seen since beginning to use virtual interviewing. As McCombs explains, "The carbon offset is just as impressive. I asked our carbon guru to do some calculations. She used http://www.epa.gov/cleanenergy/energy-resources/calculator and we found have saved close to 127,000 pounds of CO_2. That equates to:

- Annual greenhouse gas emissions from 11.1 passenger vehicles
- CO_2 emissions from the electricity use of seven homes for one year
- CO2 emissions from 6,524 gallons of gasoline consumed
- CO2 emissions from 135 barrels of oil consumed"

Waste Management has now started using this resource for more than just interviewing job candidates.

"As an added benefit, we also use this platform internally for live virtual meetings," McCombs said. "Last week I met with fifteen of our recruiters across the country who were all on webcams. These meetings are much more productive than a WebEx because everyone is much more engaged when you can see them. No one is checking e-mail—people are very present. It also helps with team development. It's an outstanding opportunity to be face to face with your team when they are all over the country."

McCombs also shared his thoughts about how virtual interviewing has influenced the candidate experience of his recruiting process.

"Based on the feedback we've received, the candidate experience is excellent," he said.

McCombs also had favorable things to say about his own experiences with using virtual interviewing.

"The level of customer service is outstanding. All we do is schedule the interview online and leave the rest to the customer service team. The candidate receives a webcam and a technical check, and then customer support attends the first minute of the interview to ensure everyone is on and things are going smoothly," said McCombs. "When we first introduced this new process to Waste Management, people thought it was cool. Now it's become the norm, and we try not to fly anyone in without first conducting a live virtual interview. I have implemented many new talent acquisition processes, and this was by far the easiest one for adoption rate and interest."

Another company that knows the benefits of live virtual interviewing firsthand is ARINC, a transportation communications and system engineering company with more than eighty domestic locations. Each year, ARINC hires about 600 people in the United States, and every person it was bringing in for an interview was costing about $1,000.

Acknowledging what a huge expense this was, ARINC set a pretty high goal for itself—reduce traveling expenses related to new hires by 35%. That might seem like a really big goal, but it's one ARINC was able to achieve in 2009 once it started using GreenJobInterview.com.

Saving money wasn't the only factor influencing ARINC and its manager of strategic staffing, Stacy Silverthorn, to begin using GreenJobInterview. Some other advantages enticed the company: being able to handle more potential applicants, reducing the number of scheduling conflicts, and being more environmentally friendly, among other factors.

Of using GreenJobInterview, Silverthorn said, "Live virtual interviews have been a huge win for us cost-wise."

ARINC has found the process to be well received by its hiring managers and candidates, showing it's been a positive experience for all parties involved.

"We now have the ability to get to candidates quicker using GreenJobInterview.com. Quality candidates are less likely to drop out due to time constraints around trying to coordinate interview and travel schedules. We can also make faster decisions, which as a result shortens our time-to-fill," Silverthorn said.

To illustrate further the impact virtual interviewing has had on ARINC, let's take a look at their award submission for an ere.net award in the "Most Strategic Use of Technology" category:[6]

---

6   Reprinted with permission from ARINC.

How has adopting new technology helped our business?

As part of an organization wide cost savings initiative in 2009, Strategic Staffing was challenged with significantly reducing personnel procurement costs. Applicant travel was identified as a large expenditure within personnel procurement. Time to Fill was impacted by internal procedures requiring a seven-day minimum advance purchase for air travel and coordination of multiple schedules (both candidate and hiring team) to confirm the interview. A routine that added a minimum of seven days to the recruitment cycle—assuming the candidate we flew in received an offer. In addition, interviewing fewer candidates meant a smaller talent pool. We conducted due diligence to secure a virtual interviewing solution that would have a positive ROI, reducing personnel procurement costs nationwide, decreasing Time to Fill, increasing the productivity of the recruiting teams and hiring managers, and providing a more thorough prescreen prior to traveling a candidate in for an interview. The result was a more efficient recruitment process, decreased applicant travel costs, improved quality of the final candidate slate, and much less time spent interviewing.

We evaluated all of the video and live virtual interview options that were on the market and determined that GreenJobInterview.com was the right solution for our needs. The level of customer service was unmatched as they provide "tech checks" for all candidates and hiring managers, had unlimited customer service support for our recruiting team—very high touch—and the consolidated monthly billing was so easy. GreenJobInterview.com offers a significant advantage over the pre-recorded video options as well as a much more cost-effective solution to live interviews that can be conducted on the WebEx Live Video or FedEx Office's video conferencing platforms. We found the solution to be very cost-effective. A virtual live interview that lasts over 30 minutes is only $99 as opposed to flying candidates at approximately $1,000 each, plus lost productivity.

There is an added benefit to this technology as the platform allows for a panel interview or a live virtual meeting with up to 16 participants. With 80 locations across the U.S., this strategy gave us a competitive advantage over our competition.

Effectiveness

Implementing GreenJobInterview companywide proved to be a major success story for ARINC Recruiting. Prior to implementing GreenJobInterview, ARINC Strategic Staffing was tasked with reducing personnel procurement costs nationwide and decreasing Time to Fill. We incorporated staffing and financial metrics from the beginning to measure the effectiveness of this new solution against these specific recruiting objectives. After implementing GreenJobInterview, our Time to Fill decreased, and our Interview to Hire ratio increased, due to the fact that we were delivering a more qualified final slate of candidates. Fifty-four percent of all candidates that completed a virtual interview using GreenJobInterview.com were hired. Applicant travel costs were reduced by 35%, resulting in a $28,000 savings in the first seven months of usage.

In addition, we discovered an unexpected ROI that was non-HR related. Remote line mangers reported a savings in business travel expenses by not having to fly in to interview candidates, positively impacting their own travel budgets and productivity. We also survey the candidates to gauge their reaction to live virtual interviews, and the response was very favorable.

Who is ARINC:
ARINC is a global company with over 3,200 employees in 80 locations. Over the years, ARINC has evolved into a dynamic, progressive leader providing engineering solutions in the aerospace and defense, aviation, airports, government, networks,

security, and transportation industries with over 150 innovative products and services worldwide. Today, we continue to support the commercial aviation industry as well as the U.S. military by creating unique, versatile innovations designed to be as optimally reliable, secure, efficient, and cost effective as possible. ARINC is headquartered in Annapolis, Maryland, USA, with regional headquarters in Singapore and London. (www.arinc.com)

As these examples of Walmart, Waste Management and ARINC show, the system works, and these are just a couple of examples. We're proud to say many other companies have benefited from GreenJobInterview and have had great experiences with us.

CHAPTER 4

What Does It Mean to Be Green?

In this chapter, Lizz Pellet will further introduce you to what it means to be sustainable and go green and how those activities are viewed by potential employees.

According to the article "A Note on Corporate Strategy on Environment Sustainability" by Piyali Nath, "environmental sustainability has grown to be the most significant area of any businesses." Nath also wrote "most companies provide committed environmental programs in order to prove to be environmentally responsible." As an HR leader, you can be directly responsible for helping implement these green programs and ensuring their success.

The bottom line is you need to know about what it means to be green and help the planet since it should be an important aspect of your human resources practices. If it's not already, you should consider making it one. Eventually, sustainability will be a must-have component of any business plan, and human resources departments are sure to play a pivotal role. By creating green practices and policies in their own departments, HR leaders can even set good examples that will hopefully encourage other departments throughout the company to follow their leads.

In 2009, Buck Consultants released the report "The Greening of the American Workplace," which examined how many businesses had green programs. Of all the survey respondents, it found 53% had formal green programs. That represented a significant increase from the year before, when 43% had formal green programs.

The survey also looked at which kinds of green programs were most popular. Recycling and paper reduction topped the list, with 95% of respondents employing these practices. Other findings included: 85% use Web conferencing or teleconferencing; 80% have healthy-living and wellness programs; 78% maintain internal green communications programs; 72% use online human resources communications; 57% offer telecommuting; and 52% have rideshare programs.

Another component of the survey was a breakdown of the desired ROI businesses had for implementing their various green programs. Of all respondents, 94% were interested in cost savings. In addition, 82% were hoping for "community good will," while 59% were hoping the programs would improve the perception held by stakeholders.

In their 2009 Green Workplace Study, SHRM reported

"20% of HR professionals work at companies that have formal, environmentally friendly policies."[7]

There are many steps you, as an HR leader, can take to make an impact and increase the number of HR professionals whose companies have policies to help the environment. The more you can think of to do, the greater the impact you'll make on the environment, and the more appealing you'll look to potential job candidates who highly value sustainability.

One way for HR departments to be major parts of the efforts to help the planet is by creating telecommuting policies. Allow your employees to work from home sometimes if you work for the kind of business where they can finish their tasks from home just as easily as if they were in an office. Telecommuting means they don't have to drive, which translates to fewer cars and related emissions. Even if it's not possible for your employees to telecommute every single day, any time they can, it will help.

Some research has shown working from home is a significant benefit to the planet. Greenhouse gas emissions could be reduced by 107 million tons per year if everyone who could was, in fact, working from home. Additionally, the country's dependence on oil from foreign sources could be 80% less.[8]

---

7   "5 Key Talent Strategies for a New Decade," iCIMS, http://www.icims.com/content/company/whitepapers/evolving_talent_trends.asp.

8   Mark Henricks, "Combine Your Green and HR Efforts: Reducing Your Environmental Impact One Employee at a Time," Enterprise, December 2008.

The report "State of Green Business 2010" said 54% of companies promote telecommuting or carpooling through office programs. According to the report, Sun Microsystems saved $70 million in 2007 alone on real estate costs.

In regard to productivity, "State of Green Business 2010" noted Cisco, which had about 85% of employees telecommuting on a regular basis, saved $277 million a year through productivity gains. The reported also highlighted Cisco "avoided the generation of 47,320 metric tons of greenhouse gas emissions" in 2008.

Working from home can also have a significant impact on employee satisfaction. In April 2011, a Harris Interactive poll from The Workforce Institute found 4% of employees in the United States called in sick rather than having to deal with their work commutes.[9] Additionally, it reported 48% said their job satisfaction was influenced by their commutes while 32% had considered the commute when selecting their jobs. Working from home would provide employees with the best commute possible, making it a very powerful incentive.

And if your employees do need to drive to work, try to set up some sort of office carpooling system. "State of Green Business 2010" reported 10.7% of workers carpooled in 2008. Carpooling is another way you can be part of decreasing the number of vehicles on the road. Make an effort to see if

---

9   "Commuting impacts job satisfaction: poll," Reuters, http://www.reuters.com/article/2011/04/25/us-work-commuting-idUSTRE73O3GL20110425.

there are employees who live close to each other so an easy route could be planned for commuting together. Encourage your employees to sign up for this system to reduce their traveling costs and their carbon footprint.

You might want to consider even giving employees some sort of incentive to participate in carpooling. For instance, maybe offer to pay for the morning coffee of anyone who is carpooling. You could also considering paying for gas or letting people who carpool come into work slightly later once a week. This will make the program that much more enticing for your employees.

Encourage the use of hybrid cars, which are better for the environment. California-based company Integrated Archive Systems Inc., gives a $10,000 monetary incentive to employees who purchase hybrids.[10] This is a human resources program serving the dual purpose of aiding the environment.

The company's founder and CEO, Amy Rao, told Entrepreneur, "The hybrid car program is such an incredible gift to an employee that it really does build allegiance to the company."[11]

As of 2008, Rao's program was so popular 50% of her workers were already taking advantage of it. Because of its success, as Entrepreneur reported, Rao even went so far as to

---

10 Mark Henricks, "Combine Your Green and HR Efforts: Reducing Your Environmental Impact One Employee at a Time," *Entrepreneur,* December 2008.

11 Rich Mintzer, "Basics of Greening Your Business," *Entrepreneur,* October 23, 2008.

extend the hybrid car incentive program so her employees' spouses or partners could also take advantage of it.

HR leaders can also create other incentive programs to encourage being green. According to Entrepreneur, some examples are providing employees with reusable bags or even giving out bicycles. Rewarding your employees for participating in the green movement is a good way to get them motivated to join and hopefully create good habits that will stay with them. And the bigger the reward, the bigger the motivation.

Such incentive programs can also help increase morale throughout the company. Happy employees who are satisfied they are being rewarded for their hard work and dedication are more likely to be productive and keep up all of that hard work.

A report entitled "Missing an Opportunity: HR Leadership and Sustainability," from the Institute for Sustainable Enterprise at Fairleigh Dickinson University, states businesses and their HR departments that are "serious about sustainability…should consider making sure that recognition and rewards are meted out for good sustainability work and the essential human and financial capital is available."[12] This is one way to help encourage individuals throughout a company to be environmentally friendly.

Another of your human resources policies should

---

12   "Missing an Opportunity: HR Leadership and Sustainability," Fairleigh Dickinson University, http://view.fdu.edu/files/missingopportunity.pdf.

involve doing virtual interviewing. Anyone who's worked in HR knows how quickly the costs can add up if you're paying people to travel for interviews. A policy of doing virtual interviews using videoconferencing will save you costs and greatly improve your hiring process.

Fi Haywood of the Virtual Assessment Centre feels there is no getting around having this type of policy in place. Haywood wrote "whether you love it or hate it, virtual and video interviewing will be an inevitable part of most company's recruitment process in the future."[13] Haywood added the positives of using this method for first-round interviews "far outweigh the cons."

With the use of virtual interviewing, Haywood said the actual hiring process will be improved, including reducing time to hire. Another benefit Haywood notes is increased efficiency. Namely, Haywood writes, it "saves us valuable time and money, which is 'tangible' and urgent."

An Aberdeen Group survey reported by Talent Management Perspectives also noted the benefits of virtual interviewing. The survey reported the length of time to fill a position was shortened by 13%. In addition, associated costs were decreased by 15%.[14]

Related to this, you also might want to consider making virtual career fairs a part of your HR department. Many HR

---

13   "Creating a Successful Virtual and Video Interviewing Strategy," HubPages, http://fihaywood.hubpages.com/hub/Video-Interviewing-Strategy.

14   Mike Prokopeak. "Lights, Camera…Interview," *Talent Management Perspectives*, February 2011.

managers have used career fairs as opportunities to connect with recent or soon-to-be college graduates who are getting ready to enter the workforce, but that's not always a cheap task. For instance, if your company is based in Seattle but you want the opportunity to connect with potential employees in New York, it can be pricey to travel to and participate in career fairs at schools there. Obviously this can all be very time-consuming too. But if you make use of technology, you can, once again, make your recruiting efforts easier and cheaper.

Unicruit explains its Diversity Virtual Career Fair allows "employers and students/alumni from some of the best colleges/universities in the country to fully interact as if in person, but from the comfort and convenience of their home or office." There are many features included in their career fair. Students "visiting" this fair can stop by your employer booth, apply for jobs or internships, submit their resumes, or even view multimedia information your company has posted, including videos or webcasts. Additionally, video interviews can be conducted, and you, as a recruiter, can chat with these potential job candidates. The fair happened live but was then up for seven days, increasing the amount of time for your company to gain exposure.

Unicruit notes young people today "live and interact in a virtual world."[15] By taking advantage of how they connect to other people all over the globe, you can enhance your HR recruiting. Use their habits to your advantage.

---

15   Unicruit, www.diversitycf.com.

While increasing your ability to reach these potential job candidates, you can also save money and the amount of time you have to spend traveling to career fairs all over the country. In fact, Unicruit explains recruiters "now have the ability to recruit at several schools at one time, but for a fraction of the cost of attending one live career fair."[16] And of course this method is far better for the environment.

It's certainly a good idea for any business owner to put together a go green plan, but HR leaders should take the initiative to look into what sustainability measures can be implemented. Outline specifically what measures you think you can take right away, and start planning out additional measures you might be able to implement in the future. Encourage your employees to contribute their ideas and make a concerted effort to find out from them what they'd like to see happen. Employees are sure to appreciate you value them enough to get their feedback. It could also help to boost morale once they know you're making changes that are important to them.

Regardless of what plan you come up with to be green in your office, there's one very important factor to keep in mind: you have to be genuine about it. Don't just say you're going to do all of these great things simply because it will sound good and will impress other people. You have to actually follow through with it all, otherwise it will just be an empty and pointless gesture. And it will reflect very poorly on you if others find out you aren't following through on your commitment.

---

16   Unicruit, www.diversitycf.com.

Being green isn't merely a way to attract employees. According to Onboarding Gen Y, it can also be a way to hold the interest of the younger generation of workers.[17] As human resource professionals, we are constantly looking for ways to engage our employees so these talented individuals will want to stay with our companies. Green initiatives are one way to maintain their interest throughout their years of employment.

Laura Schildkraut of Onboarding Gen Y points out that these individuals are well informed about environmental issues all over the globe because of their constant connections to the Internet and all the information it provides. This exposure to information, Schildkraut explains, has created in them a desire to do something to help. Your green efforts could help them fulfill this desire, thus making them feel more satisfied overall with their jobs and, therefore, will be more likely to stay.

An article by Jennifer Schramm, the Workplace Trends and Forecasting program manager at the Society for Human Resource Management (SHRM), details how sustainability initiatives positively impact the performance of employees.[18] Of 728 companies participating in a 2010 SHRM survey, 55% reported such initiatives improved the morale of their employees. Another 43% felt their business

---

17 "Engaging Gen Y in a Tough Economy," Onboarding GenY, http://onboardinggeny.com/engaging-gen-y-in-a-tough-economy/.

18 Jennifer Schramm, "Promoting Sustainability," *HR Magazine,* March 1, 2011.

processes had become more efficient. Other results of these types of programs included "stronger public images" and "increased employee loyalty."

Jeana Wirtenberg of Fairleigh Dickinson University's Institute for Sustainable Enterprise has summed up the important of being green in terms of recruiting:[19] "First of all, you'll recruit and retain better," Wirtenberg told *Entrepreneur* magazine. "Second, you'll have people who are more engaged and productive."

Recruiting high-quality job candidates can have a lasting, positive impact on your company particularly if you have strong retainment efforts in place as well. The U.S. Office of Personnel Management notes, "Getting the most valuable applicants to fill your vacancies dramatically increases the odds of retaining those employees. Placing an emphasis on strong retention strategies can help your organization retain your valuable human capital assets."

Although some HR professionals are already making their practices sustainable, research has found they are not yet as involved as they should be. According to a recent study by Fairleigh Dickinson University's Institute for Sustainable Enterprise, HR leaders "are not yet capitalizing on that opportunity [to enhance their strategic roles], even as their organizations progress toward sustainability."[20]

---

19   Mark Henricks, "Combine Your Green and HR Efforts: Reducing Your Environmental Impact One Employee at a Time," *Entrepreneur*, December 2008.

20   Joel Harmon, Kent D. Fairfield, and Jeana Wirtenberg. "Missing an Opportunity: HR Leadership and Sustainability." *People and Strategy* 33 (2010)..

However, the report concluded, "given the strong personal affinity for global sustainability issues expressed by survey respondents, the need for HR leaders to step up and play a stronger role in moving their organizations toward sustainability seems greater than ever."

Environmental Impact Reduction and Its Importance

There's no question it's important for all people to work to reduce their environmental impacts. Now that people are aware of the damage being done to the planet, many are thinking about what they personally can do to minimize it.

The Lance Armstrong Foundation explains a "carbon footprint is the overall amount of greenhouse gas admissions, consisting primarily of carbon dioxide, associated with an organization, event, or production." In addition, the Center for Sustainable Economy (CSE) defines an ecological footprint as the "measure of humanity's demands on nature."

By visiting the CSE Website www.myfootprint.org, you can take a twenty-seven-question quiz that will tell you what your footprint is and how it compares to the rest of the world. Some of the questions the survey asks are where you live, the amount of people in your household, the forms of energy and renewable energy you use, your yearly travel, your energy saving habits, and your use of biodegradable or nontoxic cleaning products. By answering these questions based on your office and even your HR practices, you can get some hard numbers about your environmental impact your company is having on the planet.

The Lance Armstrong Foundation also details several ways people can reduce their personal carbon footprint, and many of these steps can also be taken by businesses. First of all, reducing waste in the ways we previously have mentioned can make an extremely large and positive difference in addition to turning off electronics not in use and working to conserve water.

The CSE also encourages the use of "cleaner transportation." In addition to riding a bike or walking somewhere, you can also take public transportation. "State of Green Business 2010" reported only 5% of employees used public transportation to get to work in 2008. Before you travel somewhere, stop to think if you really need to drive there yourself or if you can get there an alternative way, and get your employees to think about that too. As an HR leader, you can help encourage your employees to use cleaner transportation by giving incentives to those who ride a bike, take public transportation, or walk to work.

Being green and environmentally conscious isn't just a fad or something done to appear hip; it's something important everyone needs to be active in to help the planet. A lot of damage has already been done to the earth throughout man's existence, but now that we know about it, it's our responsibility to do what we can to protect it.

Even the federal government has acknowledged this needs to be addressed. To help businesses in addition to individuals, communities, and governments, the United States Environmental Protection Agency (EPA) has created recommendations to promote environmental stewardship.

The EPA's Website explains, "Businesses and other institutions have a wide variety of opportunities to practice environmental stewardship. From the way they manage their operations to the products and services they offer customers to the projects and activities they support in their communities, businesses and other institutions can play an important role in protecting the environment and preserving natural resources."[21]

Furthermore, the EPA's Website provides environmental information based on the issues, your industry, or even your geographic location. You can find out about green issues, EnergyStar, and resource conversation and sustainability among other topics. Visit www.epa.gov/stewardship to find out what you and your business can do to help these efforts. This could help you formulate ideas for improving the green programs your HR department has to offer employees.

---

21 "Everyday Choices: Opportunities for Environmental Stewardship," United States Environmental Protection Agency, http://www.epa.gov/environmentalinnovation/pdf/rpt2admin.pdf.

The Younger Generation

People of all ages can be interested in doing something to help the planet and go green. Although it's not exclusive to one age group, it could be more of a deal breaker for the younger generation when it comes to accepting a job. Research is showing younger members of the workforce are thinking about environmentally friendly efforts when they're looking at potential employers. And recruiters will definitely want to draw in this younger generation since they are the ones who will eventually be replacing the current generation of workers.

Particularly for people who are twenty-five and under, the green movement has become highly valued. They've grown up hearing about it and being told why they need to get involved. You frequently see younger people active in the movement, including participating in awareness campaigns or actually getting out there to help with various cleanup efforts. It's a strong indication the topic is truly hitting home with them.

For Generation Y in particular, there are strong attitudes toward the link between being environmentally conscious and their workplace. "Generation Y and the Workplace," a 2010 report from Johnson Controls, looked specifically at how those between eighteen and twenty-five felt about workplace factors, including being a friend to the environment.

This research included 5,375 respondents. Of them, 3,011 were eighteen to twenty-five, 1,298 were twenty-six to thirty-five, and 396 were thirty-six to forty-five. The countries included in the report were United States, India, China, the United Kingdom, and Germany.

One of their findings? Generation Y values sustainability and "are looking for a sustainable environment offering a social structure within both a physical and virtual environment." It's not just about a job and a paycheck for these individuals; it's about finding an employer that shares their values, including the need to protect the planet. They want to work for someone who is willing to contribute to the green movement not because they have to but because they actually want to.

Of the Generation Y people surveyed, "96% want an environmentally aware workplace." Additionally, the report found 57% of Generation Y want their employers to be environmentally friendly, while 37% want them at least to be environmentally aware.

"Generation Y and the Workplace" also looked at some of the specific green measures this generation is interested in. For instance, members of this generation are in favor of walking to work, recycling, and using natural light, just to name a few examples.

About 70% of the survey's respondents said they want recycling bins in their workplaces. (Studies show employers are already doing well with this. According to "State of Green Business 2010," 93% of employees "report that they have an easily accessible recycling bin at their work.") Other findings include 47.4% being in favor of water-saving devices, 52.7% feeling offices should have standby devices for electrical equipment, 71.6% are in favor of sharing office printers, and 47% want on-site solar panels. Many of these are simple initiatives HR managers could easily help implement in the workplace to help make their employees happy.

Among the recommendations made in the report were for employers to go beyond just the minimum compliance measures. Potential employees interested in sustainability efforts will want to see you're going above and beyond. Doing merely what you're required to do won't be enough; instead, you need to take some extra initiative and think of additional measures you can implement.

Also, it was recommended employers show evidence of their green work. After all, you can't use all of this going green work to your advantage if no one knows about it. Don't be afraid to promote what you're doing. Incorporate it into your careers Website and make sure it has a prominent place in all your recruiting materials because it might just catch the eyes of some very talented job candidates.

The research makes it clear: when it comes to the younger generation, environmental issues are important to them. Employers can't ignore this, particularly if they want to be able to attract these workers. Anything you can do to give yourself a competitive edge over other businesses in your field to draw in job candidates should be taken seriously, and this is one of those factors. You don't want to lose talent because you could have been more environmentally friendly but didn't take the steps to make it happen.

Although job candidates have to show their worth to the companies they want to work for, as a business owner or human resources manager you still need to be able to attract them to your company. And if the eighteen- to twenty-five-year-olds feel you don't care about the environment, they may not even want to consider working for you. Running a business is tough enough without putting yourself at a disadvantage by ignoring factors important to your current and future employees.

Be sure to take these concerns seriously. While it might make a difference for younger candidates, it will also help your company overall. More employees will most likely respond positively to your efforts, and it will help clientele realize you care about the community and making a difference. It's a win-win situation for you. It could be good publicity for you all around as many people take notice of what you're doing.

Does HR Need to Be Green?

Lizz will now walk you through why it's important for HR to be involved in going green. She'll start to explain to you the Felix Global three-step process for making your own HR processes green and will take a look at how being green can impact the candidate life cycle.

So far in this book we covered that green is the new black. Just like organizational culture was touted in the '90s as essential for business success, social responsibility seems to have taken its place during this decade. It's good to be green—that's what a lot of companies are finding as they integrate environmentalism and sustainability into their corporate culture. Not only is environmentalism good for the community and the planet, it can help employees reduce waste and operate more efficiently. Companies tout their environmental initiatives in annual reports, core values, and community activities, but they often fail to leverage their environmental efforts into their employment brand. Many companies are missing a key opportunity here because studies show a commitment to sustainability can be a factor the most desirable candidates weigh when choosing an employer.

There are three main drivers for you as an HR professional to consider as you determine if you should create a greener organization: importance, cost savings, and congruence. The first thing you have to determine is whether social responsibility really matters to your candidates. Since green recruiting is such a new idea, there is conflicting information out there. Talent management leaders must determine if social responsibility is important enough to the top talent they seek for them to go green in order to attract and retain these candidates.

The second driver to creating a green recruiting function is the significant cost savings associated with green solutions. I am sure some may disagree with me and say this should be the number-one driver, but as the economy regains strength and companies begin to hire at their pre-recession levels again, the focus will be on finding the best qualified candidates and the right cultural fit.

The third driver is congruence. If your organizational culture touts an environmentally friendly mission or emphasizes sustainability in your consumer advertising, then you better have a sustainable HR function! Some companies make a half-hearted attempt at greenwashing. Incongruence in words and actions can be detected a mile away by today's savvy job seekers.

Now even the clouds are green! In April 2010, the US Airways monthly magazine was dedicated to going green and highlighted ten businesses that bloomed and then boomed by leveraging sustainability. It is an interesting mix of industries and proves everyone can get into the green game, save money, and increase profits. The ten featured organizations were:

- Amazon.com
- New Belgium Brewing
- Coca-Cola Enterprises
- Starbucks
- Patagonia
- Ritz-Carlton
- University of New Hampshire
- Wynn Las Vegas
- Dell
- Greensburg, Kansas

There are many ways these organizations demonstrate their green commitment, but one element they all have in common is how they have rolled sustainability into their values. This is where the third driver to go green—congruence—comes into play. If your organization sees the value of embracing sustainability for whatever reason, then it must become a value. You cannot hope to have the please consider the environment before printing footer on your e-mails and think that will send the sustainability message. Commitment in actions and stated values are where you need to be.

In a special issue of the HRPS *People & Strategy* journal there was an article on "Transitioning to the Green Economy" by Jeana Wirtenberg, senior advisor at the Institute for Sustainable Enterprise, and she called out to HR professionals with some sound advice:

> "Companies with strong reputations for having a triple-bottom-line or sustainability focus accrue benefits in several areas related to talent management, including reduced recruiting costs, reduced attrition costs, and increased employee productivity. Furthermore, 92 percent of employees "would feel better about themselves" if they worked for a socially responsible corporation, according to a national survey, and 96 percent would like to work at a "successful company that also inspires to do good." Respondents also believe that companies have an obligation to help the environment (93 percent) and that employers should support social issues (72 percent).[22]

Over the years we have been asked to continue to build competencies and move from a tactical function to being a more strategic business partner, so it comes as no surprise we will need to build knowledge around sustainability. It is no longer in the hands of just engineering, marketing, or

---

22   Jeana Wirtenberg, PhD, *Unleashing Talent in Service of a Sustainable Future* (New York: McGraw-Hill Companies, Inc., 2011), pp. 376-377.

the finance folks who love to run the numbers and report how much a company saved by eliminating bottled water and shifting to water coolers to lead the charge. HR has an obligation to participate and fully support the sustainability efforts. If HR adopts some of those great TQM (total quality management) processes, it will find a greater way to track and report out savings, and we all know how much the C Suite loves those charts and graphs. I like to take a simple three-step approach to greening up HR.

1. Evaluate—look at every step in the life cycle of the employee experience.
2. Eliminate—using solid process reengineering steps, break down these processes and remove duplication of effort, redundancy, and replace worn-out approaches.
3. Illuminate—leverage the changes you make in PR efforts and on your careers site and tout it in your employment brand.

For step one, we encourage you to perform a diagnostic on what you're already doing in terms of your employee experience life cycle. Here are some of the questions you should be asking yourself:

- Are any of your products and/or services environmentally sustainable? Really think about the work you're doing. Even if you're not in an obvious field of the green movement, that doesn't mean you're not doing something to help keep the environment going strong.

- Are there efforts to facilitate and engage employees broadly to examine operational processes and maximize environmental sustainability? It's important to keep your employees involved in your mission, especially if part of that mission is to be environmentally sustainable.

- Do you have any jobs whose responsibilities are to reduce your firm's carbon footprint? If you are, this is something you definitely want to promote as you create your sustainable recruiting practices.

- Do your job descriptions (and career Website) reflect your green commitment? If they aren't, then they should be. Don't keep your commitment to being green a secret from everyone.

- Is your firm involved in outside (community) activities to compensate for lack of sustainability in products and services? Getting involved in community activities could be a great way to illustrate your commitment to the environment, and it will also help you be seen as a valuable and contributing member of the community.

- Have you looked at your recruiting processes to calculate their carbon footprint? For those who haven't done this, there are several Websites you can use to calculate it, and it won't cost you a thing to do so. You might find it an eye-opener to see what your carbon footprint actually is, and it might end up being the motivation you need to start to change your actual practices.

- Have you been turned down by qualified candidates because of environmental issues? If so, this should raise a red flag. You don't want to lose out on qualified candidates because of something you're perfectly capable of fixing.

- Have great employees left for "greener" pastures? Where did they go? When some of your employees have moved on to other companies specifically because of environmental issues, you should put some deep thought into where they went and why. This can be valuable information. You might find it's because of reasons you can correct.

- Do your leaders know the score, and are you communicating the message? The heads of any company should be aware of the company's environmental impact and the work being done to reduce it. And the message needs to be out there for everyone to understand.

The world of recruiting as we knew it in 2008 is forever changed; 2010 has introduced a host of new virtual options and cost-saving solutions. For many in recruiting this is a welcome change and a way to generate new business by introducing these new solutions to their client bases. These solutions provide an opportunity to differentiate them from their competition. Others who continue to recruit the same ol', same ol' way may virtually disappear. Companies that do not give consideration to being green or provide just "green washing" lip service may be passed over by potential candidates who don't wish to be associated with those kinds of organizations. We see it every day. Employees are searching for authentic work experiences where their personal values are in alignment with an organization's values.

In continuing the evaluation stage, once you've answered all of the above questions the next step is for you to look at aspects of the employee life cycle and go through our diagnostic checklist. The activities on that checklist to evaluate are:

- Workforce planning
- Applicant tracking system (ATS)
- Recruitment
- Career fairs
- College-focused events

- Candidate interviews and selection process
- Onboarding
- Distribution of benefit information
- Open enrollment
- Orientation programs
- Announcements of changes in benefits
- Policies and procedures
- Performance appraisals and evaluations
- Payment processes
- Internal and external communication and PR
- Employment branding activities
- Community involvement and projects
- Reward and recognition programs
- Holiday parties and celebrations
- Corrective action plans
- Exit interviews
- Retirement benefits

After you've completed the evaluation portion of the process, it's time to begin the elimination aspect. Namely, it's time to get rid of any redundancies in your HR process and get rid of any methods that aren't working. You also have to reengineer your HR functions to be more sustainable. Don't think because something is working there's no reason to change it or revisit it. By examining everything with a critical eye, you're sure to discover areas where you can eliminate redundancies and methods that aren't working while making very positive changes in your business.

In the elimination phase we suggest reaching out to your internal quality departments as they may be well versed in total quality management or continuous quality improvement. By deploying simple quality tools such as cost-benefit analysis, process mapping, or fishbone diagrams you can quickly identify redundancies.

One area you can quickly evaluate and shift to a more sustainable and attractive approach for Gen Y is career fairs. We have seen a shift from the fifty-page printed on one side notebook to using recycled paper and printed on dual sides. A couple of years ago the trend was to move from paper to thumb drives that could be loaded onto students' laptops and then reused, but now with the shift to mobile technology and iPads (any tablet will do) we are also seeing an increase in applications that can be downloaded or scanned into these handheld devices.

Think about what it actually takes to create just one ton of paper: it's the equivalent to twenty-four trees. And it's not just a matter of losing trees. The process involves 40,000 gallons of clean water, 20,000 of which are wasted. There are also 5,690 pounds of greenhouse gases emitted to create a single ton of paper.

One of the biggest things you can do to make your recruiting process green is cutting down on the amount of travel done to hire new employees. As we've mentioned earlier, paying for potential candidates to come to you for first-round interviews can be a tremendous cost but one you can easily eliminate. As a former HR director, I love the idea of live virtual interviews. For me, the opportunity to engage in live conversation and observe body language and spontaneity with someone across the country or the globe is a great way to determine the right fit with very little legal risk. HR can save big by adopting these green solutions, and while the interview process may be a good place to start, don't overlook every step in the employee life cycle.

A white paper published by iCIMS, a popular applicant tracking system, details how ATS is being instituted as an environmentally friendly approach. This company's Talent Platform streamlines the entire talent management process and enables a paperless approach to human resources. Serving over 800 clients worldwide with offices throughout North America, Europe, and Asia-Pacific, iCIMS redefines the once paper-intensive department with its state-of-the-art green functionality. The company's Talent Platform provides clients with streamlined candidate management tools such as workforce planning, applicant tracking, and onboarding. Here is an excerpt from its white paper:

> The "green approach" can be defined as a system that enables human resources tasks to be more environmentally-friendly via web-based technology. Finding a way to "green up" will not only reduce environmental degradation, but will also make possible a great deal of profit and brand enhancing benefits for the company. Below is a list of five benefits to going green in talent management.

Tangible Benefits:

Going Paperless

HR professionals are constantly striving to improve efficiency within the workplace. However, when processes are still largely paper-intensive, the initiative is difficult to implement. The talent management program demands a great deal of paper resources detailing the entire talent life cycle from application entry to exit interview. Green approaches can actually rid the HR department of paper reliance. All necessary paperwork can be completed through web-based talent management systems, eliminating the need for paper applications, onboarding documents, performance reviews, and much more.

Reducing Internal Costs

Due to the comprehensive nature of the onboarding process, human resource professionals often assist new recruits with document completion. This is important, but the process is very time consuming. The green approach automates all documents into a user-friendly online portal making it easy to complete for recent hires. More importantly, it enables HR professionals to spend less time on document management and more time on important employee development initiatives. HR professional productivity is greatly increased, and in turn organizations reap a greater return.

Additionally, the talent management process is organized completely online by automating and streamlining all candidate and employee data. As a result, HR professionals are first, finding they do not need paper and second, do not need the space to store the paper.

Improving reporting capabilities

Utilizing green approaches to talent management often fosters better reporting capabilities. Adopting a web-based system that is inherently green not only enables companies to save countless hours wasted on manual data entry and administrative tasks, but also augments quicker proficiency results. Departmental analyses are more easily accessible allowing HR professionals to visualize the inefficiencies—including resources wasted, processes to improve upon, and overall departmental success. Web-based talent management programs streamline all candidate and employee data into a centralized location creating a fully searchable and reportable software for HR professionals to base efficiency-building decisions off of.

Intangible Benefits:

Brand Perception

According to Earthshare.org, a recent poll on green employment by MonsterTRAK.com found that 80% of young professionals are interested in securing a job that has a positive impact on the environment, and 92% would be more inclined to work for a company that is environmentally friendly.[23] What does this mean for a business that is environmentally conscious? A larger applicant pool to choose quality candidates from.
Greening Business, http://www.earthshare.org/greening-business.html.

Global Footprint

In today's global marketplace, businesses are operating in more international locations, and therefore a greater emphasis is being made on the effect of business operations on other countries. Global government has also increased pressure on international businesses to create more green jobs through greener measures.[24] Implementing

---

23   "Greening Business," EarthShare, http://www.earthshare.org/greening-business.html.

24   "Declaration on Green Growth," OECD, http://www.olis.oecd.org/olis/2009doc.nsf/LinkTo/NT00004886/$FILE/JT03267277.PDF.

a green talent management program is a healthy step towards this initiative.

Step three in this process asks you to illuminate. Once you have your green practices in place, it's time to let everyone know about them. This includes developing your employment branding and green messaging. After you have fully developed the messaging, you need to start communicating both internally and externally.

There are distinct benefits of the creation of an employment brand and rolling out that message for the entire world to see and hear. Dr. John Sullivan, a widely quoted expert on HR practices stated in the article The Many Benefits of Employment Branding:

> I have found that the primary reason why corporate recruiting managers underappreciate and underutilize a corporate branding strategy is because they have done a poor job in making the business case for investing in their firm's employment brand. You can't make a compelling business case unless you first know the possible benefits of the branding strategy.[25]

---

25 "Employment Branding: The Only Long-Term Recruiting Strategy," Dr. John Sullivan, http://www.drjohnsullivan.com/articles-mainmenu-27/articles/employment-branding-mainmenu-30/183-employment-branding-the-only-long-term-recruiting-strategy.

He is right on. The business case is key in getting the C Suite to pay attention to most anything HR related. For many of these senior-level executives, it's all about charts and graphs—quantitative data that shows ROI. You know, five years ago, when I was out speaking to HR groups around the country, we never mentioned ROI—that was a finance term. These days we all know it's the only way to be seen as a strategic partner in your company.

Sullivan's article outlines the benefits of having an employment branding program:

- A long-term impact—five years, barring any negative PR issues with the company
- An increased volume of unsolicited candidates
- Higher quality candidates
- Higher offer-acceptance ratios
- Increased employee referrals
- Improved employee retention rates
- Increased employee motivation
- Improved college recruitment
- A stronger corporate culture
- Decreased corporate negatives
- Ammunition for employees and managers
- Increased manager satisfaction
- Increased media exposure
- A competitive advantage
- Increased shareholder value
- Support for the product brand

I have found most all of these benefits to be true in working on creating congruent employment brands over the past two years.

You should also make sure all of the information is prominently displayed on your Website so those visiting it can learn more. Additionally, encourage your employees to tell others about your environmentally friendly measures. Word of mouth can be quite powerful.

Gerry Crispin, the chief navigator of CareerXroads, has noted the importance of sharing this information could have on potential job candidates:

> Employers committed to "green recruiting" recognize and embrace the broader issues of social responsibility, community involvement, environmental stewardship, and sustainability of the environment and openly assess their results at all levels of the organization. They especially realize the importance of sharing their vision and actions with employees and candidates in order to attract, engage, and influence the most talented candidates to come and stay.

Having the information about your company's green practices and making sure other people know about them will serve two distinct purposes. First of all, it will help attract potential employees who share your goals and are genuinely interested in working for you. Second, it will help weed out candidates who might not be interested specifically because of your green practices. Leveraging green in your branding efforts speaks to the congruence and authenticity of your efforts and can help you to attract, retain, and repel the right employees.

Here are a few examples of companies touting environmentalism in their employment brands:[26]

New Belgium Brewery based in Fort Collins, CO, and the makers of Fat Tire, have a clever line—they claim "tastes great, less impact" as in environmental impact. Turns out they've been getting greener and greener since 1991, and in their purpose statement they simply say, "Produce world class beer, have fun, honor nature at every turn of the business." Sounds like a simple approach, but such companies are realizing hard-dollar savings in the efforts to go green.

Here is what they say at Starbucks on its in-store brochure cleverly printed on both sides to ensure you see no white space or waste; each of the six panels explains each one of its guiding principles. This message is neither customer focused nor employee focused—just the facts and honest information on what Starbucks is, but more important, what it is not:

> We believe the mark of a socially responsible company is one that adheres to its deeply held values. At Starbucks, our values are embedded in

---

26   Lizz Pellet, *The Cultural Fit Factor: Creating and Employment Brand That Attracts, Retains, and Repels the Right Employees* (Virginia: Society for Human Resource Management, 2009).

our mission statement and guiding principles. We strive to live our values every day.

Mission: Establish Starbucks as the premier purveyor of the finest coffee in the world while maintaining our uncompromising principles as we grow.

The following six guiding principles will help us measure the appropriateness of our decisions:

- Provide a great work environment and treat each other with respect and dignity.
- Embrace diversity as an essential component in the way we do business.
- Apply the highest standards of excellence to purchasing, roasting, and fresh delivery of our coffee.
- Develop enthusiastically satisfied customers all of the time.
- Contribute positively to our communities and our environment.
- Recognize that profitability is essential to our future success.

Here are some statements from other companies' Websites:

Timberland

Our mission is to equip people to make a difference in their world. We do this by creating outstanding products and by trying to make a difference in the communities where we live and work.

We're a big company made up of a lot of small parts and incredibly talented people. We make boots, shoes, clothes and gear that are comfortable enough to wear all day and rugged enough for all year. We don't rest on our accomplishments. If we did, we'd only have ever made one waterproof leather boot.

Our place in this world is bigger than the things we put in it. So we volunteer in our communities. Making new products goes hand in hand with making things better. That means reducing our carbon footprint and being as environmentally responsible as we can.

Whole Foods

Founded in 1980 as one small store in Austin, Texas, Whole Foods Market® is now the world's leading retailer of natural and organic foods, with 196 stores in North America and the United Kingdom. To date Whole Foods Market remains uniquely mission driven: We're highly selective about what we sell, dedicated to stringent Quality Standards, and committed to sustainable agriculture.

We believe in a virtuous circle entwining the food chain, human beings, and Mother Earth:

each is reliant upon the others through a beautiful and delicate symbiosis.

Whole People

We recruit the best people we can to become part of our team. We empower them to make their own decisions, creating a respectful workplace where people are treated fairly and are highly motivated to succeed. We look for people who are passionate about food. Our team members are also well-rounded human beings. They play a critical role in helping build the store into a profitable and beneficial part of its community.

Whole Planet

We believe companies, like individuals, must assume their share of responsibility as tenants of Planet Earth. On a global basis we actively support organic farming—the best method for promoting sustainable agriculture and protecting the environment and the farm workers. On a local basis, we are actively involved in our communities by supporting food banks, sponsoring neighborhood events, compensating our team members for community service work, and contributing at least five percent of total net profits to not-for-profit organizations.

And just to add another feather in their cap, they have been ranked in the top fifty of the Fortune˚ "100 Best Companies to Work For" list for the past seven years.

You get the idea it's in the company's best interest to tout its environmental efforts in its employment brand as well as public domain information.

Social Media as a Green Approach Source Information:

Serious About Sustainability in 2010
Issue 494, February 26, 2010
By Mark Vickers
http://www.i4cp.com/trendwatchers/2010/02/26/serious-about-
    sustainability-in-2010

Interview From Anywhere:
    Live Video Interviews Are Now a Best Practice (Part 1 of 2)
Dr. John Sullivan
June 29, 2009
http://www.ere.net/2009/06/29/interview-from-anywhere-live-
    video-interviews-are-now-a-best-practice-part-i-of-ii/

Enterprise
The Cloud's Green Advantage
Rob Bernard
November 15, 2010
http://www.forbes.com/2010/11/12/energy-datacenter-enterprise-
    technology-cloud.html

ERE.net
January 14, 2009
Gerry Crispin
Staffing Carbon Footprint: 1.25 Tons of CO2 Per Hire

"The Cultural Fit Factor, Creating an Employment Brand that
    Attracts, Retains and Repels the Right Employee."
Lizz Pellet, Copyright 2009
Published by: The Society for Human Resource Management.

CHAPTER 6

Why Recruiters Need to Be More Social

After discussing the candidate experience, Theo and Greg will take you deeper into the GreenJobInterview process and show you exactly how it can help with your recruiting efforts. GreenJobInterview social media strategist Greg Scott will share some handy tips on using social media in HR. While we focus on step two of the recruiting process— elimination—you will learn how virtual interviewing can help you do so. You'll also get to hear success stories and testimonials from the employers and employees who have experienced these benefits firsthand.

Just as people of all generations are very concerned with going green, many are also highly active with social networking, particularly younger members of the workforce. Social networking can be for more than posting pictures of your vacation or letting your friends know how you're spending your evening. It can actually be an important tool used by recruiters whether to get the word out about job openings or to find out more about your job candidates.

And making use of social networking in the form of social recruiting isn't something new. Some organizations have been using it since 2007. Although some larger companies might be putting it to good use, it's not exclusive to the big guys. Internet-savvy recruiters, regardless of the size of their companies, can make it work in their favor. These forms of nontraditional recruiting, sometimes referred to as "social recruiting," can be worth it.

As Tiffany Black put it in *Inc.* magazine, "It's about engaging with users and using social media tools to source and recruit talent."[27]

However, some businesses may be hesitant to use social media because of certain stigmas attached to it. For instance, there is a big concern that using social networking sites at work will cut down on the productivity of employees. Others might fear the interactions are too casual in nature and won't come off as being very professional in the eyes of the candidates you're trying to reach. Get over it.

But really, there are an incredible amount of benefits to embracing social media. According to HR industry leader Dr. John Sullivan, "social media tools are one of the top most powerful recruiting tools."[28]

When it comes to social networking sites that can benefit businesses, the "big three" are LinkedIn, Twitter, and Facebook. Sullivan estimates "95% of all social media recruiting occurs" on these three sites. Black reported

---

27   Tiffany Black, "How to Use Social Media as a Recruiting Tool," *Inc.*, April 22, 2010.

28   "High-Impact Social Recruiting Errors—The Top 30 to Avoid," ere.net,   http://www.ere.net/2011/02/07/high-impact-social-recruiting-errors-the-top-30-to-avoid/.

there are more than 535 million users of these three social media sites alone, which can make them effective ways of increasing your candidate pool.

LinkedIn focuses more on users' professional profiles, whereas many other social networking sites tend to lean more toward the personal side. Once you create your profile, you are able to link up with colleagues and create various business connections with those who might be in same industry you are. It can almost be like doing online networking.

Black detailed some of the ways recruiters can use LinkedIn to get the word out about their job openings, including posting a job opening for thirty days at the cost of $195. The site also has LinkedIn Talent Advantage, which is specifically designed to offer tools to recruiters. You can also get the word out about your job openings by using your "status box."

Through Twitter, companies can send regular updates, including links and photos, to their followers. Of course, one of the 140-character tweets you could be sending out would be about job postings and openings, including links to your own site where more information is available. One click and a follower can go to a link for further details. And since Twitter has a search function, even people who aren't your followers might be able to come across it.

"Twitter can be powerful for small companies or a recruiter who wants to get an edge over the competition," Black wrote. "The easiest way to recruit is to tweet jobs you have available." When tweeting a job opening, Black recommended recruiters even use relevant hashtags to make their message more searchable.

Black also explained your tweets can help let potential employee learn about career-related events you might be having such as a job fair or various aspects of your company. This can serve the dual purpose of maintaining interest in positions while also helping followers feel more connected and knowledgeable about your company.

Similarly, Facebook also gives you a chance to develop a following of people who are interested in your organization and want to see what you have to say and share, including job openings you're looking to fill. And if someone likes your company well enough to want to pay attention to it on Facebook, then you already have a captive audience for job postings. Black explained that some of the ways to send out your job posting through Facebook are using the site's "marketplace," which is free of charge, or purchasing an ad that will give you the chance to target specific groups of users.

"Facebook provides easy and affordable ways to increase your applicant pool," Black noted.

The more complete the network you create, the more potential job candidates, whether active or passive, you have ready to jump on that job posting of yours. It's certainly worth the time and effort to build up strong social networking accounts and pages. As the Allegis Group Services CMO told Mashable, "Social recruiting is about getting engaged and having conversations with people before they're even thinking about you as an employer."[29]

You also have to think about exactly how many people are on social networking sites. Just about everyone in the younger generations is on at least one of these social networking sites if not all of them. In fact, thanks to smartphones, there are countless people on the Internet and social networking sites constantly throughout the day. As soon as you post something, they're sure to notice it right away and click to see what it's all about. That will all be good when it comes time to fill a job opening in a timely fashion.

In addition to giving you the chance to connect to interested parties not already involved in your business, social networking also lets you stay connected with current and even former employees.[30] Just one reason you might be interested in staying in touch with former employees is because they could be interested in returning to your company. Some of these valuable employees who for whatever reason left might want to return if they see an interesting job opening you post. By keeping your business in the forefront, they might be more likely to think of you when they decide a change of job is in order, and it brings them back to your company.

Some companies have already seen what a pivotal role

---

29   "HOW TO: Use Social Media for Recruiting," Mashable, http://mashable.com/2011/06/11/social-media-recruiting/.

30   "Dow Chemical Adds Social Networking as Latest Recruiting Tool," ere.net, http://www.ere.net/2007/08/24/dow-chemical-adds-social-networking-as-latest-recruiting-tool/.

social networking can play in their recruiting practices. In 2009, Crowe Horwath released a report that said during one six-month period, 20% of the individuals it hired were found through "non-traditional recruiting methods," as explained by an ERE article.[31] Included in this was the use of Facebook, LinkedIn, and Twitter. The amount of hires who came via social networking sites specifically was 4% during the course of eight months.

Michele Porfilio, the company's strategic sourcing leader, told ERE "that overall we're getting better candidates from these social media sources, and we have a much better ROI."[32]

Sullivan has noted the numerous benefits of using social networking as a recruiting tool.[33] When used properly, this form of recruiting could result in hiring employees who are of high quality and might "perform better on the job and have higher retention rates," he said. Additionally, it can be more financially effective and make hiring faster, among many other benefits.

There is of course also an environmental benefit to social networking as noted by Tim Warmath, the vice president of recruiting at Colt. He said "social networks such as Twitter

---

31　"Social Media Recruiting Paying Off at Crowe Horwath," ere.net, http://www.ere.net/2009/12/22/social-media-recruiting-paying-off-at-crowe-horwath/.

32　"Social Media Recruiting Paying Off at Crowe Horwath," ere.net, http://www.ere.net/2009/12/22/social-media-recruiting-paying-off-at-crowe-horwath/.

33　"The Many Benefits of Social Network Recruiting: Making a Compelling Business Case," ere.net, http://www.ere.net/2009/11/02/the-many-benefits-of-social-network-recruiting-making-a-compelling-business-case/.

and LinkedIn are being widely used to push out recruitment information and receive responses, with no need for hard copy."[34] If you're getting the word out using this method, it could reduce your need to send out printed notices or pay for advertisements in print newspapers or magazines.

While building your HR use of social networking sites and incorporating it into your recruiting processes, Sullivan notes there are several important tips to keep in mind. First of all, he says, "without a clear strategy, an execution plan, and metrics to continually improve, no recruiting effort can be expected to produce extraordinary measures." Just some of Sullivan's other recommendations are to focus such recruiting efforts specifically on individuals who aren't on job boards; to build "talent communities"; to develop trusting relationships; to look at social networking sites other than just Twitter, LinkedIn and Facebook; not being too direct; and being authentic.

Many HR professionals have already recognized this tool needs to be in their repertoires. The findings of Jobvite's Social Recruiting Survey 2010 found "83% of respondents use or plan to start using social networks for recruiting" in 2010.[35] Of the 600 recruitment and HR professionals Jobvite surveyed, 78% use LinkedIn, 55% use Facebook, and 45% use Twitter.

---

34 Jane Bird, "Mobile Applications: Devices Offer Fresh Routes to the Job Market," *Financial Times*, April 20, 2011.

35 "Jobvite Social Recruiting Survey 2010: More Than 80% Of Companies Plan To Recruit Through Social Networks In Coming Year," Jobvite, http://recruiting.jobvite.com/news/press-releases/pr/jobvite-social-recruiting-survey-2010.php.

"As our third annual survey shows, social network recruiting has become a mainstream channel for employers who need access to talent," said Jobvite president and CEO Dan Finnigan in a press release. "Job boards launched a revolution in recruiting more than 15 years ago. And now, social networks are doing the same—but in a targeted way. Through social recruiting, companies are learning they can find the best talent efficiently, without making a major investment."[36]

This year, Career Enlightenment also released some stats about how those in human resource are using of social media, which was reported about in Mashable.[37] It was revealed 89% of companies would be using social networks during their recruiting in 2011, a 6% increase from 2010.

One reason recruiters might be turning to social networking sites to try to get potential hires is because of those sites' abilities to reach additional people. Monster.com reported SHRM found "just over two-thirds [of HR professionals surveyed] say that social networking helps them reach candidates who they otherwise wouldn't know about or couldn't contact."[38] Technology is helping us expand our reach, and social networking sites are a major part of this.

In an article on Mashable.com, Sharlyn Lauby noted

---

36   "Jobvite Social Recruiting Survey 2010: More Than 80% Of Companies Plan To Recruit Through Social Networks In Coming Year," Jobvite, http://recruiting.jobvite.com/news/press-releases/pr/jobvite-social-recruiting-survey-2010.php.

37   "How Businesses Use Social Media for Recruiting," Mashable, http://mashable.com/2011/08/28/social-media-recruiting-infographic/.

38   "Social Networking: The Art of Social Media Recruiting," Monster, http://hiring.monster.com/hr/hr-best-practices/recruiting-hiring-advice/job-screening-techniques/recruiting-using-social-media.aspx.

"another very large component [of HR] is to help support and cultivate corporate culture."[39] Using social networking is one way to do just that. As Lauby explains, instead of just giving HR professionals the chance to connect with other individuals who work in the field, they can additionally connect with new talent or stay connected with former employees. In fact, Lauby reported, H&M has created a specific group just for its alumni on LinkedIn, which the company's HR generalist, Victorio Milian, described as "a potential pool of rehires." It also is a way to keep the company's brand out there and visible.

If people don't know about your company, it can be difficult for them to want to work there. By leveraging your use of social media you can increase your company's visibility, thus increasing interest in it. It's always a good thing to have even more people know about your business and the works it's doing. When it comes to job seekers, you don't want your company to be a best-kept secret.

Lauby said when creating a social networking presence, it's important to provide value to those you're connected with. Instead of it just being about what you can get out of your followers, you also want to provide them with valuable information to make it more of a mutually beneficial relationship. In addition, Lauby said, it's necessary to have some sort of system in place to measure results.

---

39   "The Future of Human Resources and Social Media," Mashable, http://mashable.com/2010/11/08/human-resources-social-media/.

In a blog article, Michael Specht emphasized companies need "clear and focused measurement" of their use of social networking.[40] By using a measurement system, it will be easier for you to tell what aspects of your social networking practices are working well and what aspects might need to be modified.

Specht explains that by using quantitative measurements, human resource professionals can get hard facts, such as whether there has been an increase in the candidate pool or even if the amount of time to hire has been decreased. In his blog, Specht shared a variety of products that can assist with this. Among them are Post Rank and FeedBurner, which measure engagement; Google Analytics to determine the amount of views your page is getting and how long individuals are staying on that page; Xinu to help find out where you rank in search results; Wordpress Contest, which also gives information on your amount of page views; and tools such as Google Alerts, Technorati, and Social Mention, which tells you when posts about things that interest you appear.[41] This could include news on your industry or mentions of your company.

HR professionals aren't using social networking sites only to reach potential job candidates—they're also using them to learn more about the individuals they might be

---

40   "Social Recruiting and Social Media ROI," HR TechCentral, specht.com.au/michael/2009/04/23/social-recruiting-and-social-media-roi/.

41   "Social Recruiting and Social Media ROI," HR TechCentral, specht.com.au/michael/2009/04/23/social-recruiting-and-social-media-roi/.

hiring.[42] An article from Monster.com explained with the increased use of social networking sites, people are growing increasingly likely not just to put personal information on their profile pages but also to let others know about their professional lives and related accomplishments.[43] This means hiring coordinators could get additional insight by taking a look at these profile pages.

According to Career Enlightenment, about 20% of employers report they conduct research on possible hires using social networking sites, while about a third of employers have rejected potential job candidates based on what they found out about them online. The same survey also found about 86% of respondents thought individuals should make their profile pages "more employer-friendly."[44] Although people might initially join social networking sites as a way to stay connected with friends and family, they have to be aware employers could be looking at the material they're posting online. Competition can be tough enough for job seekers without putting themselves at a disadvantage by uploading questionable content on their social media pages.

---

42   "How Businesses Use Social Media for Recruiting," Mashable, http://mashable.com/2011/08/28/social-media-recruiting-infographic/.

43   "Social Networking: The Art of Social Media Recruiting," Monster, http://hiring.monster.com/hr/hr-best-practices/recruiting-hiring-advice/job-screening-techniques/recruiting-using-social-media.aspx.

44   "INFOGRAPHIC: How Employers Use Social Networks In The Hiring Process," scribbal, http://www.scribbal.com/2011/08/infographic-how-employers-use-social-networks-in-the-hiring-process/.

A SHRM study released in 2008 reported "about 17% [of recruiters] use it [social networking searches] as part of their hiring process," according to director of research Steve Williams.[45] As social media continue to be a part of our everyday lives, that percentage will rise.

However, profile pages don't necessary have a negative impact on hiring decisions; sometimes profile pages have helped potential employees. As reported by Mashable, profiles on social media pages helped 24% of managers determine a person's "fit and personality."[46] You can't learn much about personality on a resume, so these personal pages can help you find out a little more about who a person really is.

Social media seems to be valuable tool and does not take up a great deal of hiring managers' time. SHRM found 52% of HR professionals spent only one or two hours using social networking each week to find out about candidates, while 29% of those surveyed said they spent from three to five hours. The other 19% spent in excess of five hours.

The SHRM study also reported of the hiring managers who weren't doing these searches, 54% said it was because "they have questions about the legality of the process."[47] But

---

45   "Social Networking: The Art of Social Media Recruiting," Monster, http://hiring.monster.com/hr/hr-best-practices/recruiting-hiring-advice/job-screening-techniques/recruiting-using-social-media.aspx.

46   "How Businesses Use Social Media for Recruiting," Mashable, http://mashable.com/2011/08/28/social-media-recruiting-infographic/.

47   "Social Networking: The Art of Social Media Recruiting," Monster, http://hiring.monster.com/hr/hr-best-practices/recruiting-hiring-advice/job-screening-techniques/recruit-

some experts think it is possible to use this without raising legal issues as long as human resource professionals take certain precautions.

Although Valeri Marks described social media as "a valuable tool in a company's recruitment" process, she noted it could lead to legal questions if it is felt recruiters have used information they came across during an online search in a discriminatory manner.[48] Although she said looking at such information can help give additional insight into job candidates, Marks said "knowing how to use these websites efficiently without accessing information that could lead to possible discrimination claims is crucial in the hiring process."

Marks wrote that a 2010 report from Microsoft found 79% of hiring managers "used social media and online searching in their hiring," although 70% reported they did not use what they found during their hiring decisions. For those hiring managers who do wish to find out more about their candidates this way, Marks has several recommendations to try to help them stay away from any related problems. First, she said recruiters should create specific policies about finding out about candidates online, including what sort of information could be considered when making hiring decisions.

Marks also said if you do decide to use online searches, you must do it for all candidates and not just some. It could

ing-using-social-media.aspx.

48 "Avoiding Risks When Using Social Media in Recruiting," HR.com,   http://www.hr.com/en/app/blog/2011/07/avoiding-risks-when-using-social-media-in-recruiti_gqo037rr.html.

definitely lead to feelings of discrimination if candidates thinks you are being selective over whom you find out about online.

Finally, Marks says it's important to document what information you do examine and when it is actually used while making your decision. This way, if a problem does come up, you can specifically show how social networking was used.

Williams, of SHRM, noted verifying any information a hiring manager finds online about a potential employee could also be an important step. Basically, you can't just assume because you see something online it's 100% accurate. "Misuse can lead to infringement of privacy or unintentional discrimination," Williams said.[49]

Just like recruiters are using social media to find potential employees, job candidates certainly are no strangers to finding their jobs through a social networking site. In 2011, more than 14 million people reported they found their most recent jobs through social media.[50]

There seems to be a good reason human resources professionals are willing to turn to social media to help find job candidates, namely, it seems actually to be working. Mashable reported "65% of companies have successfully hired

---

49 "Social Networking: The Art of Social Media Recruiting," Monster, http://hiring.monster.com/hr/hr-best-practices/recruiting-hiring-advice/job-screening-techniques/recruiting-using-social-media.aspx.

50 "How Businesses Use Social Media for Recruiting," Mashable, http://mashable.com/2011/08/28/social-media-recruiting-infographic/.

via social media."[51] Maybe this is why, as the article stated, "55% of companies planned on investing more in social recruiting in 2011."

In his August 2011 blog post, Andy Sernovitz highlighted what he called "an amazing ambassador program" at UnitedHealth Group, which helps illustrate the positive impact social recruiting can have as well as how you can get your existing employees in on the act.[52] The organization has about forty-five employees who have volunteered to participate in the program.

The volunteers are trained and receive certification to be ambassadors and are also given ongoing support. These volunteers will then post comments on social networking sites if a person announces he or she has been hired by UnitedHealth Group and will send welcoming messages. Sernovitz wrote "the company is already seeing big results, as social recruiting hires outnumber hires from channels such as job fairs and traditional media."

To help put everything in perspective when it comes to incorporating social media into human resource practices, GreenJobInterview's social media strategist, Greg Scott, shared some of his insights. He explained the abilities to use multiple contact points to make personal connections

---

51   "How Businesses Use Social Media for Recruiting," Mashable, http://mashable.com/2011/08/28/social-media-recruiting-infographic/.

52   "Andy's Answers: How UnitedHealth Group is using social media for recruiting." Smartblogs, http://smartblogs.com/socialmedia/2011/08/05/andys-answers-how-unitedhealth-group-is-using-social-media-for-recruiting/.

with potential employees and attract the most talented candidates possible will be some of the biggest benefits HR professionals can gain from using social media in their recruiting practices.

"This should greatly increase the number of qualified prospects," Scott noted about these particular benefits.

Those aren't the only benefits to be had. Scott also pointed out "if the social media is deployed across the company, it will attract talent that is a better cultural fit, thereby increasing the company's retention rate."

As beneficial as it might be for companies to adopt these practices, HR departments and professionals could face several roadblocks as they try to do so. Scott said a couple of problems could be if a company's culture is not open and trusting. Without having such a mentality, social media efforts could prove ineffective, Scott said.

"In fact, given the disruptive transparency of social media, many companies will experience highly detrimental effects in their talent acquisition efforts [if they are not open and trustful]," Scott explained. "For example, a company can no longer simply build an ad campaign around its 'green' efforts if this is not authentic, since a single smartphone photo posted to Twitter can instantly destroy the campaign's credibility."

It's not enough to put yourself out there on social media; you also have to be willing and able to share information to better connect to people and be honest with them, because not doing so could severely and permanently damage your organization's reputation.

Scott has some words of advice to share if you do want to make sure your HR's social media efforts will be a success. And you don't have to be a huge, well-known business to find success in this area.

"In my opinion, over the next few years, companies with iconic brands will have social recruiting success simply because of their popularity," he said. "However, for those other companies that are not iconic, they will have the greatest success leveraging a 'greater purpose.' Companies that are authentic and tap into the values of their stakeholders will find the greatest success in attracting and retaining the best talent."

Looking to the future, it's sure social media will be major force in the world of recruiting.

"Companies will be forced to live by a set of values that are authentically embodied by their employees. We will see fewer instances of grand-scale corruption, employee abuse, or environmental damage," Scott said. "Social media will also flatten the hierarchy; it will look more like a trellis than a pyramid. Leaders will be recruited for their ability to be inspirational, empowering, and empathetic. Over the next several years social media will become more prevalent, but it will also be less apparent."

Companies that decide it's not worth it to see what social networking is all about and the sort of impact it could make on their human resources functions are definitely missing out. As the evidence shows, HR leaders need to take advantage of this recruiting tool so they can improve the quality of the employees being brought into their companies while at the same time saving money and decreasing how long it takes to fill positions.

One More Thing on Being Social

This is Theo. I always have people coming up to me saying, "Facebook is for personal use, and LinkedIn is for business." I was in that camp for a long time, and guess what? We lost. (See the data below.) People "check" LinkedIn; they live on Facebook. As a recruiter and a company, you need to have a presence where the people actually hang out. Also, let's face it—most of our weekends are not as politically incorrect as they used to be

I saw Abby Euler of Kenexa do a presentation on social media. To me it was the clearest, most useful hour I have spent in regard to social media and recruiting. Here is what Abby has to say about social media:

> The interesting thing about social media is it's all audience driven. There are certain ages and profiles of people who are automatically drawn to Linkedin over Facebook or Twitter over Linkedin and so on. It's for that reason that truly understanding your target audience or specific profile you are trying to attract for recruiting is so pivotal. There is no one answer to the recruiting puzzle other than

knowing the right message and right mechanism for delivery. It's not Facebook over Linkedin; it's understanding the need for a strategic mix.[53]

Facebook vs. LinkedIn

750 million users on Facebook

120 million users on LinkedIn

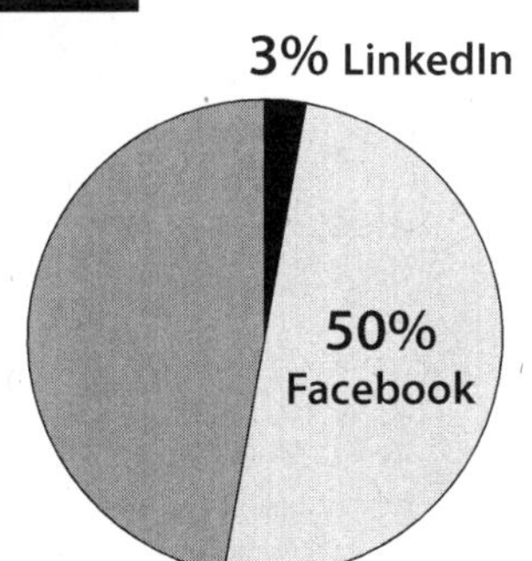

Percentage of active users

Average Usage Time

25 minutes
Facebook

9 minutes
LinkedIn

---

53   Abby Euler, phone call with author.

Getting Ready to Hire
and the Candidate Experience

When it comes time to hire new employees, it's always important to get any sort of competitive edge you can. One way to do so is by taking advantage of the economic changes.[54] Dr. John Sullivan notes competition for job candidates increases as the economy begins to improve, which means recruiters should time their hiring efforts to start shortly before this turnaround starts.

In addition to decreasing your competition for all of those high-quality candidates you're trying to nab, Sullivan explains, you can also get these individuals for lower salaries since you are not trying to outbid other companies. Getting talented candidates for less is definitely a winning combination for any business or human resources department.

To identify when this turnaround will begin, Sullivan recommends examining trends in your industry and not in the economy as a whole, getting help from forecasters, looking at historical business patterns, and looking at other job postings out there. By taking note of these factors you can prepare for the turnaround and put your recruiting plan into action before anyone else does.

Another way recruiters can get a leg up on the competition is by making it a top priority to create positive candidate experiences. Unfortunately, there are some in the

---

54　"A Pre-Turnaround Hiring Strategy Allows You to Hire When There Is No Competition," ere.net, http://www.ere.net/2011/07/18/a-pre-turnaround-hiring-strategy-allows-you-to-hire-when-there-is-no-competition/.

industry who still need to work on making this one of their priorities. In fact, Global Learning Resources founder and CEO Kevin Wheeler said he "would guess that well over half of all recruiting functions are dysfunctional" and have "no standard process."[55] Wheeler noted treating candidates poorly can leave lasting bad impressions, which can later impact a company's ability to hire the talented candidates it's after. This could either be because bad word of mouth damages the company's reputation as a potential employer or because a candidate a certain company might want to offer a different position to down the road is no longer interested because of previous experiences.

John Zappe defined candidate experience as "the emotional impression created in a person as they proceed through the process of seeking, applying, and being considered for a job with a specific company."[56] Zappe says "the better the experience, the better the hire, and the better and more valuable the employee will be." That will not just benefit businesses in the short term but also in the long term as they are able recruit valuable employees who will be interested in staying at the company for many years to come. That could also make HR professionals' lives easier if they don't have as high a turnaround for jobs and therefore fewer openings to worry about filling.

Lana Haun explains when you are thinking about your

---

55   "We Should Be Ashamed," ere.net, http://www.ere.net/2009/10/01/we-should-be-ashamed-treating-candidates-with-respect/.
56   "Pointing the Way to the Candidate Experience," ere.net, http://www.ere.net/2011/03/11/pointing-the-way-to-the-candidate-experience/.

candidates' experiences, there are certain questions you should be asking yourself.[57] First of all, Haun said to ask if "all candidates are equal," and she explained companies don't need to spend the same amount on every candidate experience since not all candidates are in fact equal. Instead, she says it should be based on the "scarcity of skill set" for a particular position.

Second, Haun says, recruiters need to look at what they should measure, including the fact that better candidate experiences could result in having better employees later on and that feedback from interviewees can help improve candidate experiences in the future. Finally, Haun said it's important to ask if "all candidates become employees" and to remember the candidate experience is important even for those who are not hired or those who might be hired on a contract basis instead of as a full-time employee. Even if you may not hire a person for a full-time position, that doesn't mean he or she won't still be talking about your business, and you want to make sure that person has good things to say.

To help improve candidate experiences, Wheeler explained it's important to create "protocols and procedures" to "lay out enforceable requirements for response time to candidates, how referral candidates are treated, what is communicated, and how shortfalls are explained to people

---

57   "3 Questions to Ask About Candidate Experience," ere.net, http://www.ere.net/2010/05/26/3-questions-to-ask-about-candidate-experience/.

who are declined." Additionally, he said recruiters must have guidelines for the amount of resumes they will accept for a given position and Websites that provide candidates with answers to possible questions that are "interactive, interesting, and enjoyable."

Sullivan has noted using virtual interviews is one way to impact positively the candidate experience.[58] He said "forcing candidates to lie to their bosses and travel multiple times is not a positive experience. It may impact their willingness to accept an offer and what they tell their colleagues about your firm."

The GreenJobInterview Process

As you start to think about using virtual interviewing in your HR practices, you're probably wondering what it involves exactly. The good news is we've created an easy process for you and your job candidates.

There just had to be a better way to do it all, which is where our process comes into play. Our goal was to change the hiring process using technology, and that's exactly what we've done.

We also wanted to create something very simple with

---

58   "Interview From Anywhere: Live Video Interviews Are Now a Best Practice," ere.net, http://www.ere.net/2009/06/29/ interview-from-anywhere-live-video-interviews-are-now-a-best-practice-part-i-of-ii/.

easy-to-use technology. Additionally, we focused on providing world-class, concierge-level support so our customer-support experience would eliminate the possibility of anyone who works with us having a negative experience. We are the first thing your candidate is going to see, and we want to make an excellent first impression. Think about that impression of being contacted by a live person versus the Skype process.

At GreenJobInterview we absolutely believe the number-one asset we can offer to those we work with is our people, and this is what helps set us apart from other companies. Anyone you come into contact with at GreenJobInterview is sure to be friendly, professional, and compassionate and will also be ready to go above and beyond to guarantee further your satisfaction. When you work with GreenJobInterview, you get 24/7 customer support we like to think of as being to virtual interviewing what the Ritz Carlton is to hotel service. Customer service is everything in our process.

So what do candidates think about virtual interviewing? We found out by teaming up with Felix Global to survey some of our customers. The survey was contacted from August 11, 2011 to October 1, 2011 and spoke with 376 respondents. Of those, 60% said they would take part in a one-way interview, while 89% said they prefer participating in a live virtual interview over a one-way interview. Another 57% said they would be willing to participate in virtual interviews that were being recorded.

What the Candidates Want!

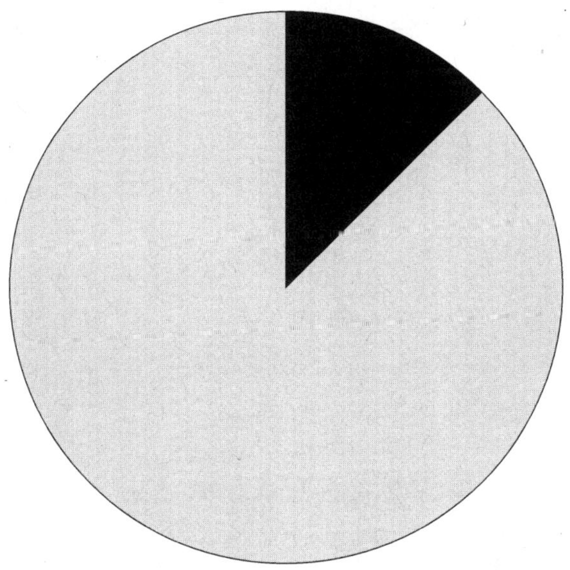

Of all the interviewees we spoke with, 98% said the company had told them in advance it would be a live virtual interview. While 38% had concerns before the interview because they were not familiar with webcams, 95% of those surveyed said they felt more comfortable with doing a webcam interview after our tech check had been completed.

A customer service representative from GreenJobInterview contacted 98% of those surveyed prior to the interview, said a tech check had been completed in advance.

About 78% of respondents said they didn't experience any technical difficulties, and 82% expressed feeling more comfortable with a virtual interview than a phone interview.

Of the customers surveyed, 81% said they had the opportunity to interview the company just as much as it interviewed them. Additionally, 79% reported appreciating not having to travel for the interview.

As with any service business, it is essential to treat all customers with respect. In fact, the way we deal with all people also helps to set us apart from other businesses out there. One of the most valuable assets we have is the ability to handle individuals in the high-quality way we do. Whenever you have a green technology company, customer service will always be the important tool you use for leverage.

Technology is all well and good, but it can't be the be all and end all. First of all, technology can have its hiccups and issues, so you need someone there to fix any glitches when they do happen. People also always want to deal with a real person when they need help using a particular technology. How many times have you called a customer service number and screamed, "I just want to talk to a real person" because you kept getting one recording after another? No one likes that feeling, and we want to make sure that experience never happens with us.

It's also the people who work for us who can help show the company's best practices and come up with solutions. All of our employees are very important to us, and we value everything they do. We're real people who really care, and we want to make sure even though we advocate for using technology, individuals still feel personally connected to GreenJobInterview.com.

Since doing virtual interviews is still relatively new, there can be a lot of confusion associated with it as people wonder what exactly a virtual interview is. Some might picture it more as a one way, recorded session during which a candidate answers questions appearing on a screen. Others think it's a two-way, live interview using an Internet-based videoconferencing solution. To clear things up: we are in fact talking about a two-way meeting during which participants talk to each other live using technology. We believe it is more valuable, engaging, and acceptable than the one-way virtual interview.

We fully understand our new clients and their job candidates might have some concerns about introducing this new step into the interview process they're accustomed to using. In any situation there's apprehension when trying something new. With the old system of conducting interviews, recruiters would review candidates' paper resumes, conduct phone screens, and then bring them in for face-to-face interviews; that's the way it was done for decades. Now, virtual interviews help introduce a new step in between phone screenings and initial in-person interviews to help ensure you really are bring in the right people.

Some people are "early adopters" and are quicker not only to understand but also to embrace our new step.

However, we find others are far more reluctant. To help address their reluctance, there are several measures we take to try to make them feel more comfortable with the virtual interview step. First of all, we help clients see the positives of this new step by showing them the many advantages of using it, which we detailed for you in an earlier chapter.

We have found some of the main concerns people have are over if the technology is going to work, how the interviewer will come across on a camera or webcam, and if they'll feel comfortable with the whole process. There are some users who have previously had bad experiences trying to do videoconferences and spent the first ten minutes just trying to get the technology to work, and those experiences have stuck in their minds. These concerns are also typically shared by the job candidates participating in the virtual interviews. Candidates want to be sure they're giving positive impressions during these virtual interviews and are worried about how they will accomplish this via camera.

First, to address technological questions while also just helping clients and customers feel more comfortable, we have our tech check service, which we consider our "secret sauce." We call everyone to walk them through the process so they can feel confident in being a part of it. We pride ourselves on having customer service representatives who are very friendly and professional.

Our dry runs with interviewers and interviewees make sure all the technology is working properly so interviews can begin without a hitch. We'll make sure candidates and company representatives won't have any troubles installing the webcams or with interview setup. Participants on both ends also get a chance to see themselves on the webcam, which can put them more at ease.

Additionally, we give pointers and tips about conducting a meeting through virtual interviews to help ensure the best possible experience can be had. We also help by making sure you have a good setup by explaining the best background and the type of lighting you need. We'll also explain how to make the best impression by doing things like looking into the camera while you're speaking. These tips can help you have an extremely successful interview.

Our work doesn't end with the pre-interview work. Instead of leaving you high and dry as the interview gets started, one of our representatives will typically join the actual live virtual meeting off-camera for the first few minutes as another way to ensure everything is running as smoothly as possible.

It's important to note in addition to making sure you have all the support you could possibly need, our process has been designed using easy-to-use technology. Even the biggest technophobes can easily use our system after interacting with one of our customer service reps. We have worked with people who literally didn't know what a USB port was. As long as you have a computer, we can get you ready to go for your virtual interview.

So what does our actual process look like? When you sign up with us, we'll give you step-by-step instructions to show you how to navigate our process, but here's a brief overview:

First, you'll need to create your own account, which will give you the ability to log in to schedule your interviews. We ask clients to schedule interviews at least twenty-four hours in advance so we have enough time to do our tech check. However, repeat users can typically schedule and conduct interviews more on the fly.

As you schedule your interview, there is certain information you'll have to enter, including the day, time, time zone, division/department, requisition number, position, and billing code. There will also be a step where you enter the candidate's information and the information for your company representative.

If you or your candidate does not have a webcam, there's no need to worry; we'll ship one to each party. So you'll just need your computer and a phone to use for the audio part of the conference.

To help with your record keeping, when you log in there is an option to create a cost-savings report at the end of each month. This will show you exactly how much you're saving your company by using virtual interviewing and will be something you can take back to show other people in your company. In addition, at the end you'll receive a copy of the Interview Request Form and e-mail invitation link you can send out to participants.

In earlier chapters we explained to you many of the benefits we're able to offer to recruiters and their companies, but there's one more we'd like to mention. A big reason clients get involved with GreenJobInterview is because of accountability. Once clients have scheduled interviews through us, they know we will be accountable for contacting the participants and making sure they are ready and the interview will go smoothly. Nothing is going to fall through the cracks, and no aspect will be neglected.

Additionally, using our company gives our clients a chance to have their brand represented in a highly professional manner. You'll also be able to promote your brand further by adding your logo, color scheme, and even your message to your "virtual meeting room" to fully customize it.

Helping Recruiters Eliminate Candidates

In the previous chapter, Lizz began to introduce you to the three-step process you can use to help make your recruiting more sustainable by highlighting the first step—evaluate. After you've completed the evaluation portion of the process, it's time to begin the second step, which is the elimination aspect. Namely, it's time to get rid of any redundancies in your human resources process and do away with any methods that just aren't working for you. You also have to begin reengineering your HR functions to be more sustainable.

For example, when it comes to your recruiting, one of the first things you should take a look at is the materials you're handing out. It could be difficult to convince people you're really all about the environment if you're wasting paper and creating more garbage. You might want seriously to consider creating digital recruiting materials you can hand out to potential job candidates or digital materials for things such as hiring packages.

According to iCIMS, a company that provides Web-based business solutions, "an organization that hires 500 new employees a year wastes more than 80,000 sheets of paper on offer packages alone."[59] A digital offering package would be able greatly to reduce paper waste.

For the materials you do have to print, first and foremost, make sure everything is being printed on recycled paper. Another thing you should do is print everything out double-sided; that way you're automatically cutting the amount of printouts by half right off the bat. (You should keep those two things in mind even for nonrecruiting printouts generated by your office.)

One of the other biggest steps you can take to make your recruiting process green is cutting down on the amount of travel done to hire new employees. As you already know, paying for potential candidates to come to you for first-round interviews can represent a tremendous cost but one

---

59   "5 Key Talent Acquisition Strategies for a New Decade," iCIMS, http://www.icims.com/content/company/whitepapers/evolving_talent_trends.asp.

that can easily be eliminated. Using videoconferencing for that first step can save you a great deal of money while also being far better for the planet than all of that traveling. Switching to virtual interviewing is definitely an important part of the elimination process.

In 2009, HR leader Dr. John Sullivan was already talking about how virtual interviewing was becoming a "best practice."[60] In fact, Sullivan wrote, "Video conferencing is not only a practical nice-to-have capability, it is a necessity for any modern recruiting organization charged with recruiting truly top talent around the world."

Noting the amount of money to be saved, Sullivan went on to say, "I predict that within a few years the 'interview from anywhere' approach will become the standard practice for all but final hiring interviews." Well it's already two years later, which means we're getting closer to seeing Sullivan's prediction come true.

Furthermore, Sullivan explained, "Using technology to reduce travel certainly reduces much of the carbon footprint and the environmental impact related to a job search. For environmentally conscious candidates, this may be a major selling point and an illustration that your company is focused on sustainability."

---

60   "Interview From Anywhere: Live Video Interviews Are Now a Best Practice," ere.net, http://www.ere.net/2009/06/29/interview-from-anywhere-live-video-interviews-are-now-a-best-practice-part-i-of-ii/.

Testimonials

We've personally seen how many recruiters have benefited from using virtual interviewing and working with us. But instead of just having us tell you about the positives, we want you to read firsthand from recruiters for major businesses about how this new tool has positively impacted their companies and their recruiting practices through the following interview stories.

Amy Rueda—UCLA

Amy Rueda, the director of strategic management at UCLA, said 2008 was the perfect time for the school to start looking at different options for exploring talent. While doing so, she explained, it was important to the university that it be done in an environmentally friendly way.

"It was just a much better use of resources for us to go virtual in exploring potential candidates," Rueda said.

It is evident that UCLA values sustainability through its many related actions. The university has its Institute of the Environment and Sustainability. Its mission "is to generate knowledge and provide solutions for regional and global environmental problems." Some of the work UCLA has done includes advising business and policymakers; conducting research; offering related academic programs; partnering with government agencies, nonprofit organizations, and the private sector; and having a Green Office Certification Program and a climate action plan.

An experienced recruiter already by 2008, Rueda said she knew virtual interviewing would be the next step to come out of videoconferencing and she was absolutely used to it. She said it was her clients who had to adjust to the new method but once they did they "absolutely loved it."

Candidates also reacted favorably to the virtual interviews. In fact, Rueda said, "Candidates love it more than anyone. They have been able to explore opportunities with us in such a confidential manner."

Rueda also said candidates like that UCLA has made its hiring process as simple as possible while maintaining privacy and efficiency.

"They're always blown away with it," she added.

Now, Rueda describes virtual interviewing as a "critical tool" for UCLA.

"We use it all the time," she said. "We use it every month."

Rueda said UCLA has become very accustomed to using virtual interviewing. For out-of-town candidates, she said, 99% of the time a virtual interview is conducted first and it is very rare for the university to bring someone in without first doing a virtual interview.

And although the tool was initially used in Rueda's department, she explained this HR resource is now being used campus wide.

Using virtual interviewing has helped UCLA in several

ways. First of all, Rueda estimates the university has saved thousands of dollars in traveling expenses alone. She also said virtual interviewing has given UCLA the chance to explore opportunities with more people and it has thus increased their job candidate pool.

A couple factors led Rueda and UCLA specifically to use GreenJobInterview. First of all, she said working with the GreenJobInterview executives who were classically trained recruiters meant they understood what her needs were and how virtual interviewing would impact her job.

The second factor was the "white glove service" she received from GreenJobInterview. Rueda added that participants on both ends are taken from "point A to point B" in a friendly and courteous manner. She also noted GreenJobInterview treats UCLA's candidates the same way they would be treated if they were to come to the school's campus.

"They're just amazing," Rueda said of GreenJobInterview's customer service representatives.

Rueda said UCLA was probably one of GreenJobInterview's first five customers, which she said gave UCLA the opportunity in the early stages of the company to tailor the service to its needs and give feedback in real time. Although there was some getting used to things during the first couple months of using GreenJobInterview, Rueda said she now feels like it's an extension of her own team.

In Rueda's opinion, the strongest aspect of GreenJobInterview's services is that its staffers are technically savvy and that they know how to troubleshoot. She said they are very well trained to handle any technical issues that might come up.

"At this point I would not consider another vendor. This is it," Rueda said. "They have exceeded all of our expectations with this product and their service. They go out of their way to meet the needs of their clients."

Mike Grennier—Walmart

Mike Grennier, the senior director of corporate recruiting at Walmart, started using virtual interviewing with a couple of interviews in October 2009 and then began to increase the volume of interviews being conducted using this method between December 2009 and January 2010.

"We live in a small town, so we have to relocate nearly all candidates we consider," Grennier explained of his Arkansas office.

For each position that needed to be filled, Grennier said they were bringing in three or four individuals to interview, which was becoming "a huge cost and time issue." He said being able to screen some candidates via video has made a major difference and made a lot of sense for the company.

Grennier compared doing a virtual interview for the first time to using Skype for the first time—at first you aren't sure about it, but within a matter of seconds you realize how easy it is to use. He described virtual interviewing as being the second-best method of conducting an in-person interview.

Conducting virtual interviews has grown at Walmart. In 2010, Grennier said, Walmart conducted 2,088 virtual interviews. He said the company is already on pace to outdo that number in 2011, having done nearly 300 in one month alone at the home office.

"It's become part of who we are; it's become part of our normal hiring procedure," Grennier said.

Although using virtual interviews is not a policy, Grennier said it is a recommendation, and use of it varies by department. He also said he thinks the success of virtual interviewing in his department has prompted other departments to take a closer look at their own work and what they can do to make it better and more cost-effective in addition to more environmentally friendly.

Virtual interviewing has made a major impact on Walmart. In terms of money, in 2010 alone the company saved more than $2.2 million. Grennier said Walmart used to spend about $1,200 for each candidate who had to be brought in, counting airfare, hotel, and car rental, among other expenses. For 2011, Grennier anticipates Walmart will save $2.8 to $3 million just by conducting interviews this way.

Using this tool has also represented a large time savings, since now Walmart is able to bring in only those candidates it feels are most qualified. Grennier additionally noted

Walmart has been able to reduce its environmental impact by decreasing its carbon footprint.

Grennier said candidates have responded very favorably to using virtual interviews in part, he feels, because of how familiar they are with using it in their personal lives. He also said candidates have been very appreciative of Walmart's approach and using virtual interviewing has shown the company cares about details such as cost and carbon footprint impact.

"It really has made an impression on candidates that we're using this as a screening tool," he said.

Grennier said the simplicity of GreenJobInterview's system is what made him decide to use their services. He described it as being "easy, straightforward," and "surprisingly simple."

"It's really the easiest system to use out there in the marketplace," Grennier said.

To Grennier, GreenJobInterview is also an extension of the Walmart brand. He pointed out that every job candidate is also a Walmart customer. So when GreenJobInterview calls a candidate to do a tech check, Grennier said, he knows that person will be treated as well as he or she would be if someone from Walmart were calling him or her.

"They're offering is not a tech solution," Grennier said. "It's a candidate-care solution."

Taking this green measure such as this also helps promote part of Walmart's overall mission. As the company's corporate site states, "We know that being an efficient and profitable business and being a good steward of the environment are goals that can work together." Three of Walmart's stated goals are "to be supplied 100% by renewable energy," "to create zero waste," and "to sell products that sustain people and the environment."

CHAPTER 7

Industry Experts Add Their Insights

To round out the information we're providing you with about being green and making your HR practices more sustainable, we spoke to some experts throughout the industry to see what they had to say about it. We share their insights with you in the following interview articles.

Toby Barazzuol *is the president of Eclipse Awards, a company that has grown a great deal since it got its start in 1998. He explained companies all over North American now use Eclipse Awards to provide recognition awards. Barazzuol said the mission of Eclipse Awards is "to really help companies recognize the people in their organization and do that in a thoughtful way." We spoke with Barazzuol about some of the top sustainability incentives he has seen businesses use and the importance of doing so.*

There are several sustainability incentives Barazzuol has seen companies instituting, including using green and eco-friendly incentive awards made out of recycled materials. He also said the "gift of time" can be a powerful incentive, whether it's an extra full or a half day off or even just the chance to come in to work a few hours late.

Barazzuol also said he's seen more people doing events and fun office projects as a form of incentive. For instance, in his own office they had a recycled-paper airplane contest that gave everyone a chance to participate and enjoy themselves.

Having in-house meals together has also become popular. Barazzuol explained these meals can be good for team building while also helping to reduce carbon emissions since employees don't need to travel anyway to get something to eat.

A newer incentive Barazzuol has seen is giving gifts or monetary donations to various organizations in the name of a specific person being rewarded.

"I think it's really important [to provide sustainability incentives] because we have to recognize and celebrate the things we value within our business and within our business communities," Barazzuol said, noting companies that value sustainable thinking must show they really do value and appreciate it.

At the moment, Barazzuol estimates the amount of businesses making use of these kinds of incentives is only between 5 and 10%, although he said that amount has definitely been growing. He explained businesses that are more progressive and leading edge are those that have really embraced sustainability and "don't see it as a flavor of the month."

Among the companies embracing it are those that already are green businesses such as recycling organizations, he said. However, Barazzuol said it is now spreading more and more in traditional businesses.

Barazzuol also said that he feels sustainability is "one of the single greatest" things businesses can invest in and that those who don't understand it now "probably won't be around in ten years."

For those who are looking to "greenify" their life cycles, Barazzuol said there are several steps they can take. To get started, he recommends looking at the resources you're using, tracking them, and starting to look at ways to minimize consumption.

Barazzuol said when you look at being sustainable, see it not as something limiting. Instead, see it as an opportunity to take those limits and use them to drive creativity while creating new products and opportunities. It may be limiting in materials in this sense but not in others. Barazzuol sees it as a way for professionals to look at their industries through a new lens and to try to reimagine their companies.

He also noted these green changes can begin with small things and then start snowballing. Barazzuol says these measures can be better accomplished when you're not kicking and screaming, adding it helps "to embrace it and understand it and figure out how to use it to strengthen your business."

When it comes to creating sustainability incentive programs, Barazzuol also shared some tips. To begin with, he said, it's important to focus on key performance indicators that align with your company's values. He also recommended using incentives in line with what you're trying to recognize.

Additionally, Barazzuol suggested professionals be creative with their rewards and make it fun and enjoyable for all the people involved.

Brenan German, the managing principal of the talent acquisition advisory and recruiting services company Bright Talent Resources, Inc., has years of experience in the talent management field. He previously was Black & Decker Corporation's director of human resources and talent acquisition for one of its divisons in addition to being the manager of global talent acquisition for Edwards Lifesciences, a recruiting technology pioneer at Directfit, and the recruiting director of The Gallup Organization. German spoke to us about where he sees green HR practices heading in the future.

In talking about green practices, German explained it places an emphasis not only on efficiency but also on the need to reduce a carbon footprint. German said where the future is heading is "very simple."

"I think you're going to continue to see the adoption of

systems to replace paper processes, and you're going to see the use of paper diminish over time," he said, noting as an example the way many people now pay bills online. German said that the same thing will happen in businesses and that technology will be favored over paper.

German added that aside from maybe finance and engineering departments, human resource departments "push a lot of paper" in order to comply with federal and state government regulations and because of the importance of having documentation. And although the move toward going paperless has already been in place and evolving, German said he thinks the industry will now see the movement accelerate.

To highlight this, German explained how going paperless is happening specifically in the hiring process. Just some of the paper that's typically been involved in this process has been used for hard copies of resumes, applications, thank-you notes, offer letters, and new-employee packages.

"You have so much paper you're dealing with there," German said. "That entire process has now been automated."

Instead of jobs being printed out and posted on bulletin boards, they're on Websites. Job seekers can apply to jobs online and send electronic resumes. German said there are even online applications that provide hiring managers with templates they can use for capturing notes during interviews among other tools. He also said even thank-you notes have gone electronic, as he's received some through text messages, e-mails, and even on social networking profiles.

Many other HR functions have gone paperless, German

said, including transfers, promotions, development plans, performance improvement, and employee data and files storage.

German said while some technology companies might be quicker to adopt such paperless activities, there is a bell curve, and other companies might take longer. However, he said, the profession is moving in that direction very quickly.

German also explained government regulations have caught up with technology, which has aided HR departments in going paperless for their record keeping. He noted "electronic signature was a big deal." Previously, although changes to the law said employee information and documents could be stored electronically as long as they were secure, a wet signature was still required. The change several years ago to allow for electronic signatures, German explained, has made everything automated now when it comes to government processes.

Human resources is currently going through a transformation, German said. He said although it was once seen more as an administrative function, it now has a strategic business partner role and it is becoming more important when it comes to business relationships. German said when HR is "truly" a part of a business, there will more likely be a buy-in to develop and implement green practices, particularly in innovative companies. However, he noted, companies that still see HR more as an administrative function will probably continue to follow the status quo.

In addition for businesses needing to view their human

resources departments as a strategic component, German said it will also be important for them to have the right strategic HR professionals in place in order to achieve innovation successfully. He also said it's important for HR not only to understand these new systems but also to accept and adopt them. One factor that could determine whether a professional does this, German said, is his or her age. He added that those who have been in the workforce for fifteen years or less are using technology and that those who love and always use technology will be the ones more likely to embrace it in their work lives.

German said it's important for there to be a catalyst present in order to push reforms and innovations at a business. If there isn't, these changes could take much more time to happen. Other factors German said could drive these changes are competition and regulations.

One of the things that will impact the likelihood of companies developing green human resource practices will be if the practices are easy to implement. German said at the end of the day no one will use a new system if it isn't easy. The other factor, he noted, will be if something is important. German explained if something is easy and important, it could be "a wonderful tool."

German also had advice for HR professionals who are getting ready to go green. "It's very important to understand how your practice works," he said. For example, he said, it's important to look at anything you do that requires paper and look for how technology can be integrated to manage the data better. In regard to the hiring process, one area where German said HR professionals should be going paperless is in their applicant tracking systems regardless of the size of their organizations. The next phrase of their going green plan, he said, could include learning and performance management.

German described green HR practices as being "huge" and "everything." Using them, he explained, can not only help remove inefficiencies but can also result in increased production and reduced costs—all while being better for the environment. He also said in addition to helping the actual businesses, green HR practices can benefit people in general as the carbon footprint left behind is reduced and diligence amount employees to pay attention to what matters is encouraged.

Social Recruiting and Social Media ROI

It is said in business you measure what matters.

The same can be said for the implementation of social recruiting/social media. Basically its use is designed to positively impact your business. The only way to ensure that this is in fact the case is through clear and focused measurement. Measurement also allows you to adjust your approach along the way. Spending too much time in one area without a positive return? Then measurement will help you understand how to make changes. Finally, measurement is part of reputation management; as the only way to understand your online reputation is to measure what is being said, it's also the only way to really manage your corporate brand online.

The measurement process does not need to be complex. However, it docs need to allow you to understand the impact on your business.

I also believe there is no right way of measuring the return on investment for use of social media in business. Why? Because the objectives for using social media are different.

Let's look at *Quantitative Measurement*. Quantitative measurement is required when you are looking to measure hard numbers such as increases in candidates or sales, site traffic, speed to hire, and reduction in calls to your customer service staff. To measure the results, you will require tools and services that provide you information on your program success.

As part of regular business operations you should have tools to measure your sales, time to hire, etc., but what about measuring your activities online and your reputation?

Here are eleven free tools to get you started:

1. **Post Rank**

   Post Rank is a free service that measures social engagement on online content produced in RSS feeds such as blog posts or news stories. This is done by measuring the type and frequency of your audience's interaction with the content, for example bookmarking, commenting, blogging about the post.

2. **FeedBurner**

   FeedBurner is an essential free RSS distribution service that provides detailed blog readership measurement and engagement metrics. Using FeedBurner, you can measure the number of subscribers to your feed, gain an understanding as to which blog posts are popular, and also measure users who have taken action based on your content.

3. **Google Analytics**

   Google Analytics is another essential tool for any web site. Google Analytics provides sites traffic trends, search keywords, conversion measurements, time spent on your site, and the number of pages viewed. Google Analytics provides a professional level of information for free in an easy-to-use and understand layout.

4. **Xinu**

    Xinu measures the status of your site in several search engines and social media sites. It also provides some simple diagnostic tools to allow you to improve your site.

5. **Wordpress Popularity Contest plugin**

    If you are using WordPress as your blogging tool of choice, installing the Popularity Contest plugin by Alex King is highly recommended. This plugin measures views; comments, etc. are tracked and provided point values to determine popularity.

6. **Google Alerts**

    Are e-mail and RSS updates of the latest Google results based on your specific watch list words or topics. You can subscribe to each alert through e-mail and RSS. The alerts track blog posts, news articles, videos, and even groups. Set a "comprehensive alert," which will notify you of stories as they happen for your name, your topic, and even your company.

7. **Technorati**

   A free blog search engine that amongst other things allows users to create custom watch lists of words of topics. When one of your terms appears, Technorati will add it to your customer RSS feed for that watch list.

8. **Yahoo Pipes**

   A free service from Yahoo that allows users to build very complex aggregation tools, called Pipes. The Pipes can be either kept private or shared publicly. Yahoo Pipes is a very comprehensive tool; however, I would not recommend it for someone without significant technical skills.

9. **TweetBeep**

   A tool that reviews the content of public Twitter updates, Tweets, and based on your key words will send you an e-mail either hourly or daily as people discuss your keyword. If your business is locally focused, the alerts can also be restricted to specific locations so you do not get over-loaded with irrelevant information.

10. **Social Mention**

    A free search engine that aggregates information across many different user-generated contact sites such as blogs, comments, photos, voting, tagging, and microblogging. Users can subscribe to the watch lists by either RSS or e-mail.

11. **BackType**

    Most of the above tools do not allow you to see the comments left on sites that might mention your terms. This is where BackType can help. BackType allows you to receive updates whenever your terms are mentioned in a comment; once again, subscribe via e-mail or RSS.

Another tip: all of these tools can be used to source candidates, plug in a keyword and "automagically" you get feeds of potential candidates. More on how to manage that information flow later. (Inspired in part by Jim Durbin's post yesterday on *Sodexo's activities.*)

There are companies having success with recorded interviews, and we would not want to leave them out of the sustainability discussion. We have included this blog post, a great overview of one organization choosing to use the recorded interview method.

How to Get the Best Talent NOW!
Advice for both employers and future college graduates on how to set yourself apart in the crowded job market

Felicia McKinney, National Campus and Diversity Talent Acquisition Lead, CDW

As the economy continues to make a labored recovery, companies are still cautious to increase their hiring. According to a survey by the Collegiate Employment Research Institute at Michigan State University, 36 percent of companies which hired new graduates last year are either uncertain they'll hire or have decided they won't hire this year. The survey found small businesses are still reluctant to hire while companies with more than 4,000 employees, or those which had preliminary hiring goals targeting new college grads, were more likely to hire in the coming year.

For recent or soon-to-be college graduates, these statistics can seem confusing as they try to find a place to start their job search. For employers with limited open positions, this means you need to ensure you are interviewing only the best candidates for each job. On campus, it's more important than ever for employers to be able to engage top talent early in their decision-making process and for students to start researching where they want to work. Some companies struggle to maintain a serious campus presence and lag behind competitors due to slow candidate engagement and outdated interview and hiring processes.

So, as a company looking for talent, how do you best set yourself up to be an employer of choice? If you are a student, how can you ensure your interaction with a recruiter doesn't start and end at the career fair table? Here are some valuable tips and tricks for both employers and college grads on how to stand out in a crowd.

Employers—Six steps to ensure you get the best talent now!

1. **Re-evaluate your current school selection list.**
    The smaller the list, the more involved you can be on each campus. Consider deeper involvement on fewer campuses rather than surface-level involvement on numerous campuses. You should be able to justify with your business partners the high yield

you receive on each campus your company targets. If you aren't able to demonstrate this result, then reconsider the school.

2. **Understand and clearly articulate what makes your organization a "magnet" for the type of student you want to engage.**
Don't make the assumption the reputation of your organization will motivate students to want to work there. Instead, highlight specific qualities about your company beyond awards and career advancement, while emphasizing the key attributes of your corporate culture to pique the interest of new applicants. An example would be playing up your company's dedication to work-life balance programs, or the different dress codes offered as part of a unique office culture. These highlights can be included in all marketing materials, both online and in person.

3. **Take advantage of social media— students do!**
Is it hot right now? You bet it is! However; LinkedIn, Facebook, and Twitter are just the basics. Consider YouTube, blogging, or even creating chat rooms to make your

company the one which students want to "stalk" online. As social media is increasingly becoming the medium many students use to search for information on a company before applying, be sure your online messaging is marketing your organization effectively.

4. **Use technology as an opportunity to make your company stand out.**

   At CDW we increase our brand awareness on campus by telling our "story" of being a cutting-edge technology company through virtual recruiting efforts… Candidates get the opportunity to interview in a comfortable setting, and CDW is able to the expedite candidate selection process without compromising the quality and consistency of selection. Some campuses are even using Skype to invite employers into their classrooms, making it even easier to connect with companies from around the country without costly travel expenses.

5. **Get creative with information sessions.**

   Students no longer care about the free pizza and outdated video presentations which were once the norm for information sessions in previous years. Think outside the box—for instance, consider hosting a mock interview session, where students can come and practice networking in a social setting with people from inside your organization. Offer stations with recruiters which can review their resumes and give tips, etc. Bringing something of value aside from your job opportunity will allow you to engage both the active and passive candidate on campus.

6. **Engage early and often!**

   How early do you start your recruitment process? Is your workforce planning built to anticipate hiring needs at least six months in advance? Are you interviewing students early enough in the year to be able to extend offers to meet revolving staffing needs?

   In today's tough market, many students are looking to receive employment well before their last semester of college. This doesn't mean you are obligated to extend an offer and get a student to commit on the spot. What you can do is while top candidates are entertaining other offers, you have an opportunity to do much more than sell the virtues of your company, give them more.

For example, allow the students to tell you where they are interviewing. Offer advice as a mentor, and always know what your competition is offering. This allows you an inside look into the students' decision-making process and the ability to help influence this decision. Set a monthly appointment to call all your offers and those you are holding for future consideration. Sending care packages during finals is also always a nice touch.

Now, students—set yourself apart from the pack!

With a national average unemployment rate of 9.6 percent, soon-to-be college graduates must be diligent in their job searches and interview preparation to get noticed. In such a compressed job market, it boils down to how good you are, not just in general but compared to the numerous other people interviewing for the same role. Being prepared for the job search process and starting early allows you to exceed an employer's expectations. This is the key to landing yourself the right job straight out of college.

Here are five important rules to follow which will help guide your expectations in order to set you up for success.

1. **Set realistic career expectations.**
   Understand the market you are entering. Do more than just research the companies you want to work for. Research your industry in general and be able to answer questions such as: Is hiring up or down? What are the average starting salary ranges? What are the top two business trends in the industry? The more knowledge you have about the field you want to enter, the more prepared you will be to engage a recruiter in conversation and understand how your experience matches the business need.

2. **Professionalism is paramount.**
   Do you present yourself with a mature demeanor and polished communication skills? Coming to an interview or a job fair with a resume and a suit are just the basics. Being able to articulate your value to a future employer in any setting will

serve you well when searching for employment. The more an employer can "see" you in front of their customers will increase the likelihood of you getting called in to meet for a face-to-face interview. Many students take the slang they use every day into conversation with employers. "Dude...yeah, like, you know" and "totally" are not for use during first introductions.

3. **Make your career search a part of your schedule.**

When you begin searching for a career, set a calendar appointment each month to engage the contacts you have made. This interaction can take place via telephone, e-mail, even snail mail. The conversation can include whatever is relevant at the time, but keep it professional. If the company recently received an award, shoot an e-mail of acknowledgement and congratulations. Perhaps send a holiday card, or call and see if there may be an opportunity for a tour or shadow during your winter/spring break.

The stronger your relationship is with the recruiter or hiring manager, the less likely your name will be lost in the pile of resumes.

4. **Consider an internship.**

   You don't know for sure what you really want to do until you've actually done it! An internship serves two great purposes. First, it allows you to test drive a company and a position to determine if you're headed in the right direction. Second, it gives you real-world job experience to discuss in an interview setting. Don't rely on your classroom projects and extracurricular activities to give you enough to articulate your value to a company.

5. **Take your time making the right career decision, then stick to it!**

   If you need time to consider other offers, communicate this to your potential employer, and set a specific date they can expect to hear from you. Saying "I need more time" is not sufficient. Once you commit to an offer, it is not only unethical to continue to interview, it can also be career suicide. The world of recruiting is much smaller than people realize. The last thing you want is your name to come up in a conversation where both employers realize they've hired the same employee.

When thinking long term about your career, you want to maintain your communication and marketability to as many people as possible. If you choose to switch employers a few years down the line, being able to call recruiters whose offer you declined professionally can be very helpful in finding your next career move.

About the author:
Felicia McKinney serves as the National Campus and Diversity Talent Acquisition Lead for CDW, a leading provider of technology solutions for business, government, and education, and health care.

Felicia is responsible for CDW's campus and diversity recruiting strategies and programs, including campus employment branding and university relationship management. She also provides counsel and direction on attracting and hiring a diverse workforce.

THANK YOU FOR YOUR SUPPORT

Thank you for taking the time to read our book.
We hope you gained some valuable knowledge.
More important, we hope we lit a spark
that will allow you to start implementing
sustainable strategies in your organization.

FOR MORE INFORMATION

If you would like more information on virtual recruiting please visit: www.GreenJobInterview.com or call 888-838-8331.

To contact Theo Rokos or Greg Rokos in regard to speaking engagements or consulting, please reach out to us at:

Theo Rokos
trokos@greenjobinterview.com

Greg Rokos
grokos@greenjobinterview.com

To reach Lizz Pellet to explore how to get your HR organization green or book speaking engagements, visit www.felixglobal.com or e-mail lpellet@felixglobal.com.